Pamela began introducing *Speak Of The Ghost* through her dramatic readings and guest speaking engagements at Antioch University, the Conference of the National Association for Women In Psychology and Jewish Women's Caucus, the Adult Children Anonymous conference, and for the Seattle Counselor's Association and healing arts collectives in the Pacific Northwest (U.S.) and western Canada.

The author extends her deep gratitude to the individuals who sponsored the printing of this book, and to those who attended her readings and presentations, requested audio-taped excerpts from and manuscript copies of *Speak Of The Ghost* and signed her guest book, as well to those whose comments are included here.

"...took me far past my usual responses to abuse issues. I love the way you expand your experiences into an art form. Great depth of self-understanding that speaks for many of us."

—Dr. Paulette Roscoe, naturopathic physician

"Pamela's poems on censoring a child's expression of self are riveting."

—Sarah Loper, sexual abuse center intern

"...helps me connect, helps me be in my body....I admire your courage in exposing your inner self."

—Diana Sill, Certified Trager® Practitioner

"Thank you for letting us in for a time—giving us a glimmer of what your path has been, the obstacles along the way, and how you creatively move through, around, over, and into them. You are brave and inspiring—I see it in your words and hear it in your voice."

—Tova Fox, writer

"...rich and evocative material...an opportunity to better understand the power of creative writing in the uncovery and recovery processes... prompted me to question my own fear of pain and how much room our children are given to feel and be."

—Anne Harvey, MSW, faculty, Antioch University Seattle

"...tapped my losses from childhood forgotten, that men don't talk about in our culture. ...tapped somewhere in me, untied a knot in me long buried."

—Barry Schiess, landscape artist

Speak of the Ghost

Speak of the Ghost

In The Name of Emotion Literacy

Pamela Sackett

EMOTION LITERACY ADVOCATES™

Seattle

Acknowledgements

Linda Wenning

Ted Sod

Myrna Pinedo

Donna Bajelis

Virginia Stout

Jo Ann Lee

Jean Spohn

Bekky Love

Gay Paulus

Suzanne Degé

Becky Gimelli

Mark Magill

Margaret Belling (alias Margaret Wilder)

Washington Lawyers for the Arts

Marshall Nelson

Howard Stambor

NewsData Corporation

The Blue Planet Café and community

Book design, typesetting, and author/back cover photography
Daniel Sackett

Cover design
Carl Bennett Design / Seattle

For information write:
Emotion Literacy Advocates™
P.O. Box 95126, Seattle, Washington 98145-2126

Library of Congress Cataloging-in-Publication Data
Sackett, Pamela.
   Speak of the ghost: in the name of emotion literacy / Pamela Sackett
      p.   cm.
   Includes index.
   ISBN 0-929904-03-6 : $15.95
   1. Adult child abuse victims–Poetry. 2. Psychological child abuse–Poetry.
   3. Parent and child–Poetry. I. Title.
PS3569.A233S64   1994   94-22099
   811'.54--dc20   CIP

Printed in the USA with soybean-based ink on recycled, acid-free paper.
First Edition.

To the stubbornly kind individual who midwifes an inestimable number of the details where I live

Daniel

artist of diversity
gentle wisdom
musical patience
my husband
co-witness
giant friend
and...

*Shadows are in reality, when the sun is shining,
the most conspicuous thing in a landscape,
next to the highest lights.*

—John Ruskin

Contents

Spitting Image

In Memory of Mute

Author's Note

December 9, 1993

It has been nineteen months to the day that I began my *emotion literacy* campaign. I had barely begun writing a series of intense rhythmic prose pieces in honor of my childhood when an artist I had met through a mutual friend suggested we do a presentation of our work together. On May 9th, 1992, I "came out" publicly for the first time as, what I termed then, an emotional incest survivor. Generating rhythmic prose found me digging much deeper into my personal story and defining it more palpably than I had ever done writing for the stage. By presenting this material to audiences, unmediated by actors, a director or myself performing as a character, I felt exposed. That evening my colleague and I took turns reading and between my pieces, I literally tremored—coming out was frightening, new and energizing. I had little more than an inkling the pieces I read marked the beginning of a yearlong creative research process entitled *Speak Of The Ghost*.

Inspired by the May 9th event, I continued ardently documenting my childhood feelings through my rhythmic prose and discovered new ways of being with myself. I began to move more deeply into old feelings triggered by current relationships. It became so much more obvious how, when I was unwilling to make room and time for childhood-based feelings, convoluted interactions persisted and kept me from feeling comfortable in my own skin, blocking my abilities to get close. Allowing room and time for feeling reversed those familiar consequences and introduced me to parts of myself that I never knew, or simply forgot, existed. I was writing and crying at the same time—this was a profound occurrence since I rarely cried and comedy writing was my forte. I had collected lots of data about my childhood and teen-age history and although I drew from this data to write music, plays and monologues, it was as though I had learned nothing until I physically felt the feelings that had transpired during those times. Depicting my history through song and script-writing did not require me to *feel* much of anything. It was, largely, work of my mental body. Although the information I tracked was useful, I had no real sense of how incomplete it was until I began to engage with it physically. The more I accessed my feelings in this way, the more I knew and understood what my history really meant to me—and then, I felt like I knew everything.

To experience these old feelings while writing was an eye-opening event because it launched me into a different way of knowing my self—my emotional body. It was coming into focus, at long last, increasing my depth of field a thousand-fold and my writing hand was rendering its portrait. With each bold stroke, my investment in bringing my emotional body back to full life grew and my whole sense of myself shifted, dramatically. Looking over the pieces in this book I see how I am perusing my feeling terrain, clearing space, clearing my throat, quaking, delineating, admitting, expressing, soothing, witnessing my emerging and previously defenseless selves and carving out a mentality to support them. I was radically clarifying the way I experienced my current relationships, circumstances and world view by viscerally connecting them to my past with no holds barred. With discipline, determination and pure curiosity, I was able to overcome the single most insidious barrier—long held repressive familial, social and religious conventions. Had I "honored" such conventions by, for instance, "forgiving" my parents, I would have remained locked into an acquired pattern banning my emotional truths and, in effect, disallowing their full bodily consciousness.[1] Luckily, I trusted my creative writing process because I had relied on it, in numerous forms, for twenty-four years. With the enlightened works of Alice Miller providing complete permission for true feelings, commencing to free myself from culturally-sanctioned constraints and my own compulsive repetition was a tissue away. Chronic physical symptoms began to disappear as my willingness to be with my feeling self grew. I was housing my emotional body in a way it had never been housed before. I was making space for it unlike my parents, teachers or society at large had. I was building my home and the words I was committing to paper became my blueprint. My "inner child" became a metaphor for my inner life and for the first time, I felt utterly qualified to be response-able for it—early life in *The Waxing Cord*, teenage life in *Spitting Image* and a synthesis of past and current life in *In Memory Of Mute*. By writing, largely, in first person, as though my emotional or feeling parts were their own person, I established direct identification with them. A detailed, rigorous and vigilant effort was required to focus on and nearly exclusively speak from the parts within myself that had long been neglected. Through this identification I prevented myself from reverting back to old, automatic ways of being: disavowing a triggered feeling, projecting the feeling onto my husband, a friend, stranger or circumstance and then suffering my old patterns of dissatisfaction and the reappearance of physical symptoms. I could nip them in the bud as long as I was willing to defy conventions, sustain direct mental and physical identification with my feeling self and ride the next wave.

I became emotionally limber. Crying became a powerful medicine for my dis-ease. I became more fluent in reading, comprehending and *having* my feelings by deciphering the unique context out of which I first learned to deny them. I was becoming emotionally literate. During this time, I began to know, beyond a shadow of a doubt, that repressed feelings become haunting entities until they are embraced, expressed consciously through the physical body, understood and corroborated by the mind. To liberate these ghosts was the ultimate spiritual experience because it was my key to self-communication.

Nowadays, repression and the resultant disavowal of the emotional body sticks out like a sore thumb—when I resort to it myself and when I notice others doing it. Having understood how the disavowal mechanism operates in my own life, I recognize how disavowed feelings get projected onto *other* individuals and groups and *other* circumstances. I recognize how the *other* always carries the stigma and as long as the projection persists the stigma prevails. Emotion illiteracy prolongs and compounds confusion and turmoil. I see how, given group support, this mechanism perpetuates itself like clock-work with destructive consequences on a grossly large scale—so gross as to obscure personal responsibility. Although many people feel free to criticize figures of authority in politics, commerce and the media, a minority of people are willing to call into question the most personally linked, original authority figures—parents. This is still taboo in most places. The moral code of consensus reality demands the flock obey without question as children and forgive, understand and, in essence, continue not feeling as adults. I *understood* my parents' problems all during my childhood. This did not prevent them from negating and censoring my emotional reality and their own in the name of parenting. I adapted to survive. But I know first-hand how that censorship dampened my most vital function—to feel. To continue to allow myself to be controlled, especially subliminally, by people who were and still are afraid, unable or unwilling to feel and integrate old losses, as well as by my own internalized and fear-propelled censorship, was no longer necessary to my survival. How I truly felt about things could be brought to my awareness and my predecessors called to account—precursors to ending the multi-generational cycle of emotion illiteracy. To have decided my parents *did the best they could* and left it at that would have been to continue negating my own feelings, and, consequently, to suffer the great loss of self-knowledge and autonomy. It would have also conveniently prevented me from moving into uncomfortable and disturbing feelings. But, through a series of phenomenal incidents of clarity, having those feelings in lieu of chronic illness became a desirable and accessible option.

Up until that point, many of my physical symptoms and life difficulties, both major and subtle, had been relegated to a *that's life* philosophy—a rationale I learned from my parents long ago as a way of masking the fallout of repressed feelings. The success that came with my initial feeling work gave me the incentive to perceive that subliminal loop of resignation and, with continued success, I began dispelling the paralyzing fear that fuels it. A new sense of confidence emerged around two very essential facts: consciously having and directly expressing my feelings is no longer a life-threatening prospect, and not having and not expressing my feelings is. To physically feel, speak about and understand past feelings and how they figure into current circumstances is not only entirely safe, it is my sturdy, incomparable and trustworthy road to real respect, choice, root self-esteem, vital growth and intimacy. By writing this book, I created a supportive mental framework within which to develop my capacity to consciously feel and, in large part, catch up with myself.

It is out of compassion and love for the parts of myself and others that suffered restrained expression that I wrote this book and want to see it in print. Supporting and being heard by those who endeavor to awaken makes going to print valuable. For me, speaking up diminishes the parallels between my current life experience and the repressive system under which I spent my childhood—mute and at odds with my true feelings. Call it abuse or emotion illiteracy but the results are the same: less breathing space and more rapacious detractions from what could otherwise be a communion with all living entities on earth, full of new surprises, free of repetitious plagues. The path to self-awareness is not a smooth course and currently there continues to be more support for staying repressed. Resignation hides out in childhood fear-based *value* systems stubbornly woven into the fabric of many cultures. But the fabric of resignation is unravelling as people become more familiar with this transformative path redefining the human condition from the root.

I am outraged by the rampant disavowal of feelings on the planet evidenced by the victim/abuser-based stories in news, film and television. I know there is much more to life than victim and abuser scenarios. My first experience with these scenarios was in my childhood home and then I carried them, like a virus, into adulthood. Through the writing of this book I traced these dynamics back to my early childhood states of powerlessness, overtly and covertly exploited vulnerabilities and unmet needs. Are not powerlessness, exploited vulnerabilities and unmet needs an ongoing theme of unrest all around the world? These conditions do not manifest out of thin air. As long as feelings of vulnerability, most commonly associated with abuse, go disavowed from childhood into adulthood, scapegoats will remain in great demand no matter how culturally diverse we seek to become. Being fully aware of and expressing the emotional body is something as children we were taught to fear. Not admitting the damaging effects of this *lesson*, or forgetting that it ever took place, we as resigned adults estrange our vulnerabilities and unmet needs. We do this through subtle forms of imposed and internalized censorship, including numbing substances and activities, victimization, and false power structures of money and status, to name a few. Without *moment-by-moment* admission to ourselves and others that we were taught to fragment our feelings and needs as children, we will teach, encourage, reward and, make no mistake, command others to repeat the fragmentation along with us.[2] To continue unconsciously repressing and projecting our childhood-based anger, vulnerabilities and unmet needs, individually or collectively, may seem expedient in the short run especially to those who find it *profitable* to do so. But emotional body censorship cumulatively wreaks havoc on individual relations and planetary conditions and perpetuates the insidious cycle of illiteracy. Over the long haul, unconscious repression and projection dooms us all to an endless road of re-cycled feelings expressed through violent or negligent acts, physical maladies and a plethora of less visible outcomes between these extremes—many of which are illustrated in *Speak Of The Ghost*. For me, it became absolutely necessary and increasingly desirable to recognize how my rashes of anger and physical symptoms acted as a last resort communication and the door to my vulnerabilities, needs and grief. The more willing I was to open it, the more favorable my association to these natural states of being and the less likely I was to expend vast amounts of time and energy tending to the fallout that descended upon me every time I resisted them.

It is insanity to expect people to care about themselves and each other on a planetary level when self-caring, in a majority of places, is actually discouraged. To have been taught, from the beginning, that only certain feelings are permissible is to be taught that some feelings are wrong. Not only does that condemn a good lot of the natural self and deter communication but it originates one of the greatest drains on human resources—the exhaustive battle between two primal needs—being true to oneself and fitting in with a group.[3] Scores of writings extoll the virtues and necessity of self-love, and with good reason. To be told that some feelings are wrong is to be dissuaded from that love. To have recognized such barriers and begun removing them has returned me my birthright—the freedom to love myself, in essence, to love life. The diligent efforts I am making to know myself exact me that freedom, evolving with it a humane, auspicious and most powerful inner authority—one that permits me to feel what I feel when I feel it; one that I hope is communicable on these pages to accompany you as you continue finding and affirming your own.

—Pamela Sackett

P.S. Although each piece is a movement unto itself, each is predicated on a previous revelation building a context for what is to follow. In that sense, *Speak of the Ghost* is a story with a beginning, middle and end, occurring within a measured time and space.

Due to the nature of my writing process and my history of writing for dramatic interpretation, *Speak of the Ghost* is geared to an oral tradition. Reading pieces out loud to yourself or another will infuse the words with emotions' fuller meaning and might prove to be of added benefit.

Footnotes

[1] For a more complete explanation of why forgiveness is problematic, please refer to Alice Miller's *Banished Knowledge* (pages 133-34, 151-54) and *Breaking Down The Wall Of Silence* (pages 33, 35, 36, 48, 58, 117, 125, 130-36, 140, 141 and 158).

[2] I say moment-by-moment because emotional truths are a constant factor in routine daily life to be denied or acknowledged. The emotional body is a constant companion, a constant reality, whether we recognize it or not. There is always a choice—to consciously feel or not feel what is truly within given any and every scenario. We can either continue the legacy, accumulate more backlog or open to a more fluid range of life experience.

[3] The original group I needed to fit in with was my family and fit in I must were I to survive. Since repression was the rule, being true to my emotional experience was hardly an option, especially since my models were not true to theirs.

Speak of the Ghost

In The Name of Emotion Literacy

The Waxing Cord

*A Poetic Uncovery
for the Emotionally Incested*

Dedication

Keep silent about it
or
spill your voice
I was taught to be mute
keep silent
or
shout it
spill your voice
or
never, never, never refute

So what if I wake up
and my voice goes tumbling
all over town?
what if I take up
the choice to go rumbling
with undeniably audible sounds?

Town Crier
born in '51
in Muted, USA
"They're liars!"
what if I say it
what if I take my bag of words and display it
for pay
"It was a farce—my childhood!
That'll be ten dollars please.
It's a farce—my childhood!"
I'll sell my wares
and then I'll pay you back I will
I'll divvy up the shares
here's one for those who gave me heartache
and threw me off a cliff
if they hadn't I wouldn't have words to sell
sometimes I think I wouldn't be well
but for words
greater than my own breath
great enough to break my fall

and now if you don't mind
well, even if you do,
I have to tell it all

or do I?
am I compelled to sell my words?
can't I just speak them to myself?
I must keep them away from those who, when they hear it,
would rather we stay on the shelf
those reminiscent of a training deficient
instructing me not to speak
is selling my words an act of rebellion
or a cycle I need to complete?

I'm a writer and I sell words
herds and herds and herds and herds
why should these be any different?
these that galloped even harder
these that took me by the hand
these that held me close and rocked me
and wielded the ultimate high command
over unspeakable emotion
over my own drought and my own famine
over co-habitants of a chaotic land
my words rose up to take the stand
testifying for me amidst turbulent commotion
where sentences blankets be
to those who need that kind of warmth
borrow my words from me
don't take them though
for that I fear
will leave me again hungry and dry
without words
I only have left to say
what and where am I?

U-Haul

What do you do when you're eight years old and your sister has a seizure and your mother cries in your hair brush and your father calls you princess and your parents hang their hopes and dreams around your neck with an inoperable clasp, a thousand pounds of silver, a million tons of rust and they tell you you're special especially when they need you when you come downstairs and walk across the mine field that someone calls your home, what do you? What do you do when your parents say you're special and your sister wants to kill you or render you inoperable and your mother tells you she'd go on a slow boat to China with your whole life ahead of you and with your whole life ahead of you, you tie up your shoes and put on your jacket and walk out the door and walk down the street and pray when you get there, her mother will ask you in and Gloria will be sitting there, eight years old, on Diet Rite Cola and saltless saltines, and you give her a smile and reach for the freezer door and liberate six fudgesicles.

They were cold in that freezer. Alone in their box. Brown and gooey and alone—with your name all over them. Six. Count them. Six. Six on a stick. One at a time in your mouth down your throat with the help of your u-haul hand sitting on your eight-year old knees. At the table in a chair next to Gloria. She calls you the bottomless pit and doesn't mind that you're half her size. Her father owns a grocery store. There's plenty for everyone.

She

Who is this woman?
this breastless woman
this dry-nippled
fleshless
skin and bones of a woman

Who is this woman?
this rageful
put on a pretty faceful
help me! help me! woman

Who?

Who is this woman?
in my closet clouds
with her siren loud
she is screaming to you
she is screaming for you
she is screaming in you

Go!
get go you woman!
you hungry, hollow shell of a woman
with your hazel eyes as big as the sun
you were my everyone
you were my mother
you were my lover torn
my lover worn out by the world
left
with vengeful scorn
and in her vengeful scorn
it was me who was born
her daughter

"You were planned," she said
I was planned?
in her head
neck up!
neck up!
neck up!

not down
numb loins
numbed groin
how in hell could she conceive me?
never to believe me
and my shocking reflections

I was joy
not her
I was joy personified
I was beauty
not her
I was gold
I was everything she couldn't have or hold

I was everything she wanted
and more
and more
and more
'til she laid me down
under the granite floor
and said
"Here, hold this.
I'm going out for a while
to drink and to dance.
You don't mind," she said
"you can wait for me in my garbage bed
and cover yourself with my hopes and dreams
first let me wrap you up in my twisted schemes
they will warm you
like my burning madness bones
jarring, tarred in a fire
keep it going!"
I'm her daughter for hire
"Keep it going!"
I'm her daughter
her kill
I am her daughter
still

who is she?
and where on earth is *my* will
who is she?
help me! she holds it still
who is she?
who is she?
I have had my fill

Rabid Tale

Jump up daddy
jump up high
like a dog who hears his name
jump up daddy
jump and fly
where'd you learn to be so tame?
jump up daddy
your hind legs hit
your hind legs kicked me over
jump up daddy
we jump the same
I'll close my eyes
who takes the blame?
while you chase your rabid tale of shame

jump up daddy
she's calling you
she's calling out your number
jump up daddy
jump and sit
while your other daughter throws a fit
and winds her confusion around your heart
do you have the strength to pull it apart?
no!
and I don't either

jump up daddy
we're all in the kennel
awaiting a compassionate master
the incumbent fed us poison
and fed herself some too
but her antibodies lasted longer
they downright outlived you

jump up daddy
I'm growling loud
I'm growling now
can you hear me?
we didn't have to jump so high
we didn't have to

No More

Don't take me under your wing
for I am not a gentle thing
I am gentle no more
and I am not your obeyer

Don't take me under your care
for we are not a pair
and I'm not going anywhere
with you
anymore

Don't take me
don't take me

for takers I have known
are takers to be sure
they take you under pretenses
"mother," "father," "sister," "uncle"
take me 'til I'm sore
take me
take my core

I gave it to them
before I knew it
I gave it
they took it
before I grew it

I gave it to them
the older, the bigger
so naturally I did
so naturally I gave it all
to the older, not wiser
the needy, the needy, the need-disguiser
at the time

I wasn't even walking
at the time
I wasn't even balking
at the thought

I never could think it
how the takers, the takers had to drink it
combing the desert
high and low
their thirst forced them to kneel down so
they could hold me
I was young
they could hold me
I was a tiny one
they did hold me
they held on for dear life
while they rocked their own ghosts on streets of strife
my Lithuanian grandmother paved the way
the umpteenth mother-pure
she suckled the wall of darkness
her daughters suckled her
and I mine

So don't take me under your wing
for I want to be an independent thing
I want to fly and soar
I want to break free from your broken wing
and hold onto it no more

As I Go

Excuse me, please
I have no etiquette
I'm clumsy as I go
but if I don't blow your cover
it's me that's going to blow
and I can't do that to myself again

Pardon me, won't you?
I have no etiquette
my manners are kaput
but if I don't let *this* fire burn
my own life will turn to soot
and something in me wants to keep glowing

I'm sorry, sort of, but, no, not really
it wouldn't be really real of me to conceal
what we do
I want to be real
I want to breathe
I can't kneel down and seethe and swallow
this starchy, cardboard fare forever
did you think I could keep silent about this secret that we share
this endeavor
this lie that says I'm not I
I'm not me
I'm you
I'm you
I'm through with burying the fool
the child that lived once for your smile
and paid for it with her tender body
her tender body so small
and her open heart that consumed it all
like a mammoth iron girth
I suggest you take a wider berth
while I unstrap myself and heave you off
and ditch this lock-up beat
I have found my own voice
the one I speak

the voice that feeds me life-support heat
the voice
excuse me
that don't sound so sweet

Note

My story has no rhyme or reason
but please let me tell it
my story was not born of your season
your storms cannot quell it
although I know you've tried
you've bounced your ball of pride
and admonition
and begged me to go chasing after it
you've trounced on my insides forcing my journey
the long way around
I never meant to confound your frozen heart

I just want to, need to
please
let me tell this story
my story
and guess what?
it's not for sale
or yours to impale
or yours to shrink
or yours to wallow in
or yours to own
so don't wave it like a flag
your arm's too short
it's motions lag
and stave my story off onto creased pages
of your own making
my story is not up for taking
down the numbered aisle
to the measured weight
impound your guile
this is my story
not yours to file
not yours to crunch into a fist
beyond recognition
don't flex your wrist
you cannot grasp the point
the gist

of my story
this is my story
I have to tell it

And what is it?
what?
it's not color-coordinated
that's for sure
it's not approximated by your eye
your tunnel eye
don't funnel my story down the tube
because you fear the giant cube of derision
my story cannot be told by omission
or by running away
or running toward
your arms
are as stiff as a board

My story is like a blanket with a cord
I pull it around me
and I hear its resounding note
my story!
my story!
it keeps me afloat

Insatiable Seed

It was my turn to feed the family of three
the family of three plus one
my turn from the beginning
my plus not to shun

I dished up something cooking
behind the shadow of the heat
I dished up without looking
at this ambidextrous feat
I dished out bowls of wonder
and bowls of I'll never tell
how I juggled the family appetites
and made mine disappear so well

It was my turn to feed the family of three
the plus one will have to wait
the family of three is hungry now
I parked *my* hunger at the gate
and served up three squares from out of the errors
saving up the insatiable seed
to sprout in my own secret garden
of I am here to please

The family of three is a triangle
the plus one a dot in the center
that lines up across the corners
to balance the starving mourners
draped in white like a table cloth
that shows its every spill
I wipe it up with one hand
with the other I pay the bill

The family of three is my crowning glory
good customers
fat pride
the family of three is my company
my symphony inside
and oh how discordant
how utterly discordant

we've played out of tune for years
how did this family go from out there
to deep inside of here?
and how do I digest a meal now
without the family gear?

From Now On To Me

What can I do for you, mother?
I'm at your beck and call
It's not that I'm unselfish
it's just that I'm too small
to run away
I tried once
I got as far as the mailbox
and when I returned
you hadn't even noticed that I had left
your needs were scheduled elsewhere that night
my plan was less than deft
I'm still trying to get away
a way out

What can I be for you, mother?
a special daughter for your elastic dreams
that stretch beyond my pliant seams?
but I never even noticed
that I had any of my own at all
it's not that I am ignorant
it's just that I'm too small
and connected to you
I'm still trying to find a way
a way out

What can I see for you, mother?
I see with your eyes too
I see no vast horizon
I see only black and blue
I see whatever you need me to
it's not that I am blind
it's just that I can't find
the door to outside of your octopus room
please stop hugging me into your solitary gloom
I want to see further
I want to see out

What can I learn from you, mother?
that anticipation is sweeter than reality?

your waiting room spins in a void
and every magazine I read there
spells out how annoyed you are and have been with life
I wish I had a gentle knife to cut away your sorrows
to sever all your yesterdays
that bleed into my tomorrows
I want my days to be my own
I want my days now

What can I say to you, mother?
and how many decibels are required?
for you to really hear me
do you even have to hear me?
for me to begin to steer me
from dawn to my own dusk?
it won't be with *your* tusk that I dig myself out
of what you are and have been about
to unearth the separate and the stout of me
do I really have to shout
or do I just walk away quietly?
I'm really very small when I try to walk away
I'm smaller than I'm smaller than
my feet are made of clay
ready to be shaped in my current year
before your residuals spike and sear all my love
what's left of it
is promised
I really have to promise it from now on
what can I promise, mother
first
to me?

I Never Knew

The silent scream has a deafening blow
a silent scream is telling
the silent scream is a heavy boat to row
a silent scream needs shelling

"A fifty-two year old man
who loved life!"
that's what everyone said
so what was he doing lying and stewing
in a Mt. Sinai hospital bed?

The silent scream has a deafening blow
a silent scream is telling
the silent scream is a heavy boat to row
a silent scream needs shelling

A fifty-two year old man for the first time
was crying
I wiped his tears and brow
A fifty-two year old man had, for years, been lying
to himself and us somehow

The silent scream has a deafening blow
a silent scream is telling
the silent scream is a heavy boat to row
a silent scream needs shelling

A fifty-two year old man, my father
who never learned to bother
with the pain that he held deep
until it all collected
in his hushed-up, cinder sleep
did he think we would have objected
to knowing about it?
did he have to re-route it
into an early demise?
just one whimper from this man
could have shaved it down to size

The silent scream is a deafening blow

a silent scream is telling
the silent scream has a heavy boat to row
a silent scream needs shelling

A fifty-two year old man
a husband
and a favorite son
and a devoted brother
who entertained everyone
he entertained with his curtain-dance
delighting all partakers
he looked at me with his childish glance
I never knew he was such a faker
I never knew his child
his very own
his child, inside, forlorn
I never knew
he never spoke about
the little one tossed and torn

The silent scream has a deafening blow
a silent scream is telling
the silent scream is a heavy boat to row
a silent scream needs shelling

A fifty-two year old man
said come out to play
to everyone but himself
a fifty-two year old man
lived for fifty-two years
with his hurts stockpiled on a shelf

A fifty-two year old man brought it down with a slam
unmistakable
for all to see
I have pain, he said
I'm in over my head
and it's overwhelming me!

The silent scream has a deafening blow
when the silent scream comes calling
the silent scream is an overload
it killed him to do the hauling
alone
in my darkest hours
when I visit his echoed cries
I think of my father
with whom I conspired
to bury the child with our stealth
but the child
long ignored
always evens the score
by taking much more than your health[1]

The silent scream has a deafening blow
it could be just a ripple on the water
"Let it out, let it out, let it out, let it flow!"
a fifty-two year old man said to his daughter

Chidehood

What do you do when your mother wants to be famous and she puts you on hold while she builds her billboard with broken sticks and papier-mache and she puts you on hold every moment every day the phone rings she flaps her lips and sings for the washing machine listen Bogart and Bacall look-a-like I wanted a bike that year you gave me a flat tire while she pumps herself up to the television set drunken visitors pretending they all had movie contracts go to bed kid and play in busy traffic what do you do?

What do you do how do you do that I can't paint your billboard with my blood anymore sit me in the corner I need you in my playpen throw your indecision dresses in the air with my bottle warm my bottle better give me plastic nipple is not better Dr. Spock who said that she was afraid of her baby she was afraid of her baby she was afraid of her baby fame and fortune around the corner pass my corner again and I'll pull you down but I can't reach you want to be famous is that it you always wanted to be famous instead of having me over your barrel of fun freaks in your circus of flailing con artist advertisements larger than life you want to be larger than life? You are to me!

What do you do don't you want me to dance for company any more you want to dance yourself dance yourself give me lessons will you I know how to be a child of yours is not is not will not be not be be my mother *first* before everything else is blaring shut off the TV you don't look like me dye your hair again and maybe an agent will come knocking on your bubble head contracts aren't made for housewives take a chance don't lose romance with one man in a crowd of groping strangers.

What do you do when can you do motherhood the myth motherhood the movie motherhood the fable read me into the corner over here over here she's climbing up her billboard again she's going to fall off again she's going to forget me down here again the monsters are coming the monsters are coming they're going to take away your billboard with you on it and then what oh my god there's a snake in the corner trying to get me to tell your billboard to stop talking so loud you can't hear me. Ride away on your billboard Miss miss miss I don't miss you I don't need you remind me not to need you that I can do it my I'm a good girl I'm a perfect girl I'm a funny girl I can do it all myself I can do it all myself myself myself in the corner the walls are closing I can close the walls hold the wails away from too close the walls I can I can I am the wonder child I won't disappoint you like her. She disappoints you and your billboard while daddy is at work jerk jerk jerk my sister around her body is a twisting mass of disobedient flesh *I* will mesh into your five year ten year twenty year plan to be famous and fortunate for having me compared to your other daughter compared to the contrivance caught between the kicking leg last leg of your mismarriage miscarriage of needs flicked into your temples your scalps your rhinestones are blinding I can't see your billboard I can't hire your billboard I can't pay your billboard I can't hug a billboard. I can hug me I can do me I can be me and you are a team fill your washing machine full shining tries try try try try try try try to get by on individual lives cannot be sold in the media ashamed in the shadow of can't measure up in the fifties only so many stories got in get in here and glue up my sticks build my sticks and stone house behind the billboard quivers in the east wind west wind middle wind in your eye has a cataract now foggy billboard is blowing away in the lonely woman on the back of a magazines cost free subscriptions are for nubile next generation billboards don't distract me I'm trying to get to you. I'm trying to get get get your attention at-t-t-t-t-tension in my head in my bed in my billboard what is this billboard doing in here oh my god it's falling on me every time I get excited I remember her billboard is stuck in my stake in my heart I can't breathe when you climb up on my back to get a better look at yourself every time you get excited I cower in the corner where are you going away away every time you get invited to your masked ball I am divided I am you am me am you am me and you I remember when you threw me in the corner to run after your billboard now *I* run after your billboard let me live the small underpopulated life no reporter gets into my life his meal ticket is not my concern I don't want to get into that restaurant anyway I don't want to get excited breath excited breath excited breath breath slow breath doesn't have to don't do run don't run every time I remember I remember I remember.

Slow I will take you down low to your frowning clown when she walked away from you drooling schooling tooling around 5, 10, 12, 15, 22, 8, 8, 10, 1, zero, minus zero minus one two three hero sprouting up from the ground crack in the dry, withered earth sip the water make the water muddy rudder sweep the gutter of your pain in the brain of your recollection tame your bitter reflection of yourself in another time another space chase chase don't chase after that echo perches on the opposite corner from where you heard it once and once again and again and again take the bend around to around through and by and past the narrow corner and comb the weeds out don't yank the weeds don't tip the weeds don't tromp the weeds look at the look at them lay down in them and feel the flowers in the patch of weed song sing along take the throng and lead it you can bead it into a warm moat a warm swarm yourself in recognition of that position that before that before you could walk away you can sit down now sit low in your solar plexus knows where your anger and fear and apprehension grows feel it in your toes and your heart knows and your head out to the hammock and rock yourself rock yourself home you build your home now with rose petals clear out the nettles, rose petals in the belly hold the belly mold the belly to your every wish now wipe the brow of the race its over over you don't have to encase yourself into the sacrificial din you can learn how to begin with to begin with splice it together in you are you humming gentle drumming gentle is gentle is is what you need.

To Be

When I was seven, they wanted me to be cute
I kissed her in the basement
with my lips pursed and my ears wide open

footsteps on the kitchen linoleum
dinner cooking in the pot
dinner smells aren't better than
this neighbor girl and what we've got
down here in the basement
sneak around, sneak around
dinner smells wafting
sneak around, sneak around
don't let them find out
your body has a secret wish

tap dance to the dinner table
tap dance to my room

they wanted me to be—
she wanted what I had to give
warm body in the backyard
warm body in the attic
warm body in the bedroom
they wanted me to be cute
dolls are cute in the bedroom
I'm no doll with porcelain skin
I'm propped up with giant pores
knock, knock let me in

I want your body
and I want yours
I am seven

when I was seven
they wanted my cuteness to continue
when I was seven
I knew something was missing
I knew something was forbidden
I knew something was something I had to have
stolen

"Lay with me," she said
she was ten or twelve
or just bigger
she had breasts
I had no mother
when I was born
just after I was born
she was bleeding in the hospital
she was gone
when she came back
she held me
with her fingertips
at arm's length
at arm's length as long as a ladder
I had to climb
and when I got to the top I was seven
I was with Trisha
and her smell
and her breasts
and her skin
I puckered my lips
let me in
there's something in
there's something in me
a hunger
I can't be cute when I'm hungry
I can't be cute but I'll try
is anyone home?

Where's Trisha?
down the basement
down the basement
where Trisha smells
I curled up
where Trisha smells
under the arm
my nostrils flared

my nostrils burned
the damp walls blared
be quick about it
someone is coming

Inside Out

When I was eight
I knew cute well
I knew cute got me something
I knew cute and helpful got me more
I knew cute, helpful and talented got me something
extra plus
admiration plus envy
attention plus angst
expectations plus abandonment

when I was eight
I had cute down
I had helpful squared away
I had talented on the rise
I had cold, bitter envy from my own mother's eyes
I had a hungry lion on the loose
ready to eat me from the inside out
I knew what be-cute-or-I'll-kill-you
be-cute-and-I'll-kill-you was all about

I wanted their approval
I needed a roof over my head
I wanted them to need me
I had an appetite
I wanted true affection
I had a collection of techniques on display
I'm still trying to exchange them

Jewel-Eater's Fork-in-the-Road-Feed-Toll
Or
Feelings Charge The Censors

"It's a no-win situation," she said with a grin—toothless, jagged-lipped and festering—"No win! No win!"

She looked so very familiar. Her words were vintage music to my ears. I've seen that smile before (pasted all over my own front door). "Come in," I said "and tell me more about this losing battle—you seem so very sure of yourself. You seem to know the cure. You seem to have all the answers to all my questions and future doubts. You seem to know what life itself is absolutely and completely about."

"Permit yourself the open air," she said while leading me into the closet. "Curl up small, very small in there. Make yourself comfortable in this lovely, tiny, taut space. You can do it." She seemed so pleased as I squeezed and squelched my face.

"Permit yourself a quiet dwelling—no muss, no fuss—and pay no never mind to that swelling—hush! hush! I will take care of it all for you, so long as you're quiet as can be. It's a no-win situation. We'll get along fine if you agree. You say you have jewels very valuable? That's nice," she said with a squint. "Swallow them whole and forget about it! Jewels are best not to wear but to stint. They hurt my eyes," she whined. "Too shiny, too sharp and too reflective—believe me when I tell you I am the one, the only and most objective."

With that she closed the door behind her on my baby finger's nail. She said this space was comfortable? How come it feels, oddly, like a jail? She said to ignore the swelling—my jewels were bulging. Is that what she meant? I peered through the keyhole in the closet door and saw her back bone bent. I saw her combing her ragged hair as she paced the floor like a rat. I saw her wincing and gasping out there. Was she anticipating a ferocious cat?

I saw the room fill up with toothless others—they all grinned just the same. I saw her turn towards the closet and then I heard her call out my name. "Are you ready to come out? Have you swallowed your jewels? Are you ready to join us?" she queried.

"I swallowed my jewels—the ones close at hand, but I am beginning now to worry. I feel sick. Did you know that these jewels, when swallowed, cause tremendous indigestion? I don't think they're meant to be swallowed like this. I think they're made for the outward dimension."

"You'll get used to it," she cringed. "Now lay down in your bed and when you're all used to it, I'll let you come out. You can take your place among us soon—as soon as you dance to our toothless tune on our jewel-swallowing short-cut route!"

I leaned in towards the keyhole to continue my plea about what I thought jewels are made to be, about what I thought of jewels as food—their unsavory flavor, rough texture—so crude. Just as I opened my mouth to speak I saw the room getting dark and bleak. I saw the room outside my closet fill with more toothless grinners and I saw their leader leading them all—a jewel-swilling, hapless no-winner. I saw the lot of them, dull and demented, deteriorating from what, I didn't know. "Keep swallowing," they belched. "Keep swallowing!" They all lined up in one long straight row. They all looked green, pale green. What made them this way? I was bound and determined to know.

I was also supposed to join them. I didn't want to stay in a closet all my days, but I didn't want to turn green either. I was caught in indecision's haze. There must be another option. There must be another room. The one I could see through the keyhole was clearly an option of gloom, and a no-win option at that. No-win—that's a clear-cut future—no questions, no doubts as to what it's all about so long as one rule is followed—the one saying jewels are not made to light the way—jewels are made only to be swallowed.

I could swallow some more because more were coming, but it was harder and harder to make them go down. One day maybe it would get easier. One day maybe no more would come 'round.

One day maybe I'd look like them—I always wanted to fit in. One day maybe I'd turn pale green and develop a toothless grin. One day maybe I could get out of this closet as soon as my behavior satisfied.

"One day is never gonna come!" a jewel rolled up onto my shoulder and cried. "One day you'll learn that with us you'll win and without us you'll certainly fit right in to a place with barbed wire borders, to a place with predictable losing outcomes and inflexibly cruel, cold quarters. So swallow me, go ahead, and see what you'll get—they got theirs—those pale green creatures—no wins, no ways, no wheres, full days of losing battles for the jewel-eating preachers."

"Who said that in there? Who said that?" She pressed her eyeing eye to the keyhole. "I hear a rambunctious voice, very unctuous. It's trying to lead you astray. Don't listen to that voice you have but one choice: to swallow it and make it go away!"

"I'll swallow you instead," said the jewel, off my head it bounced and then melted itself through the keyhole. I leaned forward to see what was bound to be—the jewel eaters' fork-in-the-road feed toll.

The jewel had an obvious advantage. The jewel-eaters hadn't a prayer. The jewel was too big too swallow. The jewel-eaters squealed out "No fair! You've grown too big for us to ingest, too big for us to contain."

"And you've grown too small, too sick from it all," said the jewel. "I'll not tolerate one more invective. I'll not tolerate your telling the one and its swelling that it has but one objective. You've left me but one thing to do—to be her last meal resurrective."

With its voice blasting forth, the jewel-eaters vanished into a fine and luminous dust. The jewel vanished too and so did the keyhole I peered through and so did the walls that came between us. I was out of the closet and out of my head, not believing what I had just seen and what I had just heard was more than

34

inferred by a jewel in all its brilliant insistence. What I had just heard was a value incurred and more valuable than the highest remittance.

"Eat not the jewels that emerge from within," spoke the jewel of itself through the ether, "because jewels that are swallowed cannot shine in the hollow and what's more they will give you a fever. What's more, the green people don't know what they're talkin' about with their open air false promises and join us song. Never try to fit into a fit that time and again feels so invariably wrong. Let your jewels speak out for you unmuffled. They are maps with a surprise-a-line story to tell. If you try to eat them, well, it's like putting gum in a bell, dirt in your shirt, plaque in your heart—it's like clogging up a drain. If you eat jewels what you'll get is fearful, constricting pale green people on the brain!

Dream For My Animal's Transformation

I have an animal inside of me
and it wants to eat
it wants to devour emotional meat
my animal wants to tear it up into shreds
and then it wants me to turn what's left
to a bed
that's some kind of futon
an old futon
a very old cotton futon
without any spring
I can think of a lovelier thing to lie on
but not now
my animal is hungry now
and I have to mix it
fresh blood emotions
I have to fix it
I have to throw my animal some meat
I have to offer it up
the alivest treat
that I myself alone can cook
to meet that hungry stare
that look
that says, "Feed me now
your wild bearings
are looming large
toward an unknown field
cut them quick
take the earliest yield
don't let them grow over there too long
that kind of food tastes all wrong
and it will hurt you!"
my animal says

my animal is a connoisseur of sorts
and it knows
just what to do
to keep my crops in check
it oversees a variety of emotional strains

I come from a long line of crop-growers
an ancient tribe of carriers
baskets and baskets of emotional meat
carted and served
the more baskets the merrier
my family goes way, way back
all my relations had hungry animals to feed
and all my relations could cook
so cook they did indeed
and they passed along that favorite old family recipe
the dish that nearly prepares itself
good for ravenous animals
secure in the fact
there are heaps of it on the shelf

Some day maybe my animal will sit
and patiently lick its paws
after traipsing around this storehouse of mine
and fine tuning its terrible claws
I want to tame my animal
I want to teach it how to heel
one day I'll sit my animal down
and tell it how I feel—

Give me a chance
I'm hungry too
you trained me good so I'd carry you
from your last to your next meal
how many more succulent fruits for you
am I going to have to peel?
Slow down, move over
look out there, I'd say
and then I'd point a finger
I'd break a family tradition—
I wouldn't for another second linger
I'd head for the hills
I'd head out and away
before my animal knew what hit her

I'd take my emotional meat on that day
I'd eat it myself
just to quit her
she runs me ragged
she runs me down
if she had her way
she'd run me out of town
and hold me hostage on her island cave
she'd chain me up
she'd make me save
every last morsel for her
every last crumb and dripping
she's a glutton she is
and would rather not share one speck
for one second's sipping
I could starve her out
the barbarian
or lay her down in my bed
and pray *she* sleeps for a million years
her name is Fears
I'll call her instead
and then I'll get my shears
I'll clip back her tendrils to shorten her climb
that'll shrink her down to normal size
smaller than that would suit me
and smaller still at last until
not a soul on earth could rebuke me
for wanting to serve my own animal
up into its very own jaws
for wanting to watch my animal
eat its own self up raw

In the future
maybe sooner
my animal will grow obedient
and be content to lay at my feet
I'll say—
Fears

you've found your place
and your hunger
grows in fair proportion at last
a small bowl will do
on occasion for you
a few crumbs for my guardian's repast

From Cutting To Waxing

No more cutting
that just isn't the way
wax the cord
stretch and stroke it
no more cutting
you decided one day
emotional un-cest is a delicate operation
relax the cord
wrap and soak it
wrap and soak it
wrap
you broke it
in
into your own
your own you do
your own, your own
through and through
the strap of time has unleashed you
waxing the cord has released you
and split the memory pod
of spatial lords and merciless gods
gone
your size two feet
gone
the tight-rope beat
years of tenuous balance
gone
gone the venomous chalice
gone
drink
of your sweet self
now
you've got the cord in you
you've got the choice
the new
anything you want to do
anything
but the familiar

Eulogy For Change

Wonder child
doesn't want to get up today
her winged feet are tired and sore
she flew a million miles
yesterday
jumping fire hoops and more
she hid the moon while others were at play
she swept the rocks up off the shore
wonder child worked for little pay
a paper thin cloak of hope and pride—
her masters' blink—
a piercing look to say
her silence vow was their death defied

death of what?
and whose life was hers to save?
if her own joy and truth could rise no more
it was death for *her* to live in their enclave
to scrimp her own skin
save tears to pour

after a long and lonely sleep
they will wash her
they will awaken her at last
her heart will thaw
as it beats the claw
scraping out the years gone past

the years they wrapped her in a shroud
and applauded her out loud
for being their favorite child
the years they called her their wonder
no, it's no wonder
she was the one most easily beguiled

now the wonder child needs rest
she needs comfort, safety, love and understanding
she needs to be soothed from the shock waves of deception—
echoes of false love commanding

commanding her to kneel
to bend
to do for others as well to fend
to bow
to perform
the dance of veils in a landslide storm
commanding her to serve
to cheat with those whose cheating had long since been denied
to watch her family's illness grow
out of that death again and again defied

death of what?
she ran from it
year after year
whittling down the wonder child
into the hall of shortened breath
where noxious fears are running wild
and survival steered her to be a trader
to join in
a masquerader
in exchange for food and shelter
in that atmosphere she sweltered
but she didn't sweat a drop
the wonder child fulfilled the bargain
she never once asked them to stop

today the wonder child is weary
in her big old body
grown
today the wonder child must speak clearly
to keep from ravaging her own
and death must not be defied ever again
for in this death her feelings rise
a welcome change knowing no resignation
a front row seat in her fearless eyes

A Prayer

I'm building a grown-up nine stories high
with arms as strong as steel
and hands that can bake a pie
with legs that run like greased wheels
but that stop on a dime to cry
I'm building a grown-up to suit me

I'm building me a grown-up
wider than wide
with bones that bend to greet me
and carry me inside
with blood that flows like a river
in whom I can confide
I'm building a grown-up who likes *my* kind of ride

I'm building me a grown-up
who'll never make me wait
who'll give me time right now to breathe
and time to contemplate
who'll know just when I'm hungry
which part of me needs to eat
who'll lift me up when I'm winning
not just when I suffer defeat
I'm building a grown-up to keep me company
for *all* the times

I'm building me a grown-up who listens
with unconditionally fine-tuned ears
who sees me when I'm coming
who rocks away my fears
whose kindness knows no boundaries
whose shoulders are like a fort
whose patience lasts longer than long
and thinks anything less is unpardonably short

I'm building a grown-up who loves me
and knows that love is tenacious
and that love is required to be so
because my appetite is voracious

and knows that we stand on equal ground
and if not
knows how to help make it level
I'm building a dreamboat grown-up
who'll let me kick and scream and revel

The Distance

I am the pain you cannot see or hear
or think of or touch
or taste or smell
I am the pain that lives in restless sleep
an unremembered tale to itself tells

I am the pain that hides in the crack
of a pasted, crooked smile
I am the pain that rides on your back
and goes the distance mile after mile

I am the pain stored in your cells
wall to wall
cover to cover
I am the pain
prudence's refugee
wiping its feet on the face of your lover

I am the pain that rings just like a bell
on odd-numbered days
at unexpected times
I am the pain that reverberates only too well
uneven rhythms
automatic chimes

I am the pain that hardens in your chest
and grips your throat
and squints your eyes
I am the pain that bellows like a bull
too hard to pull
too stubborn to be chased
I am the pain that keeps your dance card full
too scared to be blank
too bold to be erased

I am the pain that keeps coming to visit
like a crude and belligerent ghost
irreverent of the facilities
the other guests
and the host

I am the pain that keeps on fighting
to re-do a battle that's long since been lost
I am the pain that until it is felt
will exact an exorbitant cost

I am the pain that once was a friend
a fitting ally
for some old state
I am the pain that lives in suspended animation
released only by a generous rebate

I am the pain that you must notice
like a thief with a backward stride
delivering jewels, a wealth beyond compare
if you dare to face that which you chide

I am the pain that turns to pleasure
transforming gasps into relief
I am the pain that upon noticeable arrival
will turn you over like a leaf
will turn you over to vast possibilities
ungaugeable
pain that surfaces leaves empty space
pain that comes becomes uncageable
with every squeeze of your arms' embrace

Ouch!

I saw her yesterday and I said, "hi"
I wanted to say ouch
I wanted to say ouch
but instead I went out of my way to walk with her

we talked and she didn't hear me
she was busy trying to get me to—
listen to yourself
listen to yourself
I said ouch
I didn't hear me and I didn't feel me but she looked so very very familiar
I kept walking with her
I slowed my pace to keep in step to keep in step
but I bit my tongue I gulped my tongue I wrestled my tongue
shut up I said shut up to my tongue to my brain to my pain
we walked some more
I told her I was writing a book about emotional incest
she said, "what?"
she said what?!
she said, "what do you mean? I make my daughter keep her room
clean
we like it tidy
we like tidy in our house
is that what you mean by emotional incest?"
I said, "more subtle than that
but that's a good metaphor for it"
she said—
I said ouch she doesn't understand she'll never
understand
I better write a book about it I better
keep my mouth shut
ouch I stubbed my soul I walked a little faster
I wanted to run
she said she went out of her way to keep up with me
we walked some more
I wanted to run I wanted to run to a clearing
to get away from what was nearing
I told her I felt uncomfortable

it's a long story but
I don't think she gives a shit about me
we worked together but for me it wasn't
a business proposition
I put my whole heart and soul into it and I got attached
because
she was so very familiar I get attached
to a certain type of behavior I get attached
like a nail digs into sticky foam
guess who's the foam?
she hired me to work for her just like someone I know
a close relative
a very close relative who I needed—
the "M" person
I can't repeat it
but survival made me blind
it made me work
it made me blind again and again and again
it keeps me blind sometimes I trip over myself and kick
myself
for letting myself or needing in myself to walk with her who
wants me to be her mirror I need to know where *I* stand in here
in the nice one minute gone the next
nice and gone doesn't rhyme with me
I disappear when she wants me to be she don't rhyme
hold on to this line don't rhyme don't make it
neat
and tidy
my feelings are about to implode and I don't even know it when I walk
with her and she says what she does is done because of something *I* did
that's emotional incest in a nutshell in a crazy nuthouse shell
I can't live in this
space any more with my face on the floor stop rhyming stop walking
with her in uniform steps its the squash army the squashers I'd rather be
squashed than left but I'm both I *was* both I was squashed and tossed
and I had nowhere to go but back to the barracks and the mess where I
sat on a spoon and the "M" person ate me physical survival sole survival

and survival of my s-o-u-l toll for survival my whole survival depended
upon pleasing her
have I impressed her yet?
have I impressed her no really I want to
impress her so badly
ouch! ouch! ouch! I wanted to impre—
im—im—im—press-press-press-press-press-press-press-press-press-press-
press my myself I want to be her circus that comes to town and dazzles
her so completely that she will never never never leave me need me need
me don't need me don't need me because that bleeds
me but stay stay something warm and sweet stay and all the rest
go! rhyme day rhyme rhyme day that's my
someone committed a crime alarm
someone is coming to come to harm me again someone is coming to split
my face my body my guts right down the middle
and then demand acquittal

one day I went walking and I saw someone who looked very very
familiar and I cancelled myself out
in advance
on the next step she said, "don't we have to compromise?"
I said, "if *you* want dinner at 5:00 and he wants it at 6:00 and you eat at
5:30 that's not the kind of compromise I'm talking about I don't think I
can explain emotional incest" describing a thing is not the thing itself
in how many tongues can I talk about the shelf?
the shelf life
the package that I became the shelf and the package are the same
sometimes I'd rather go insane than try to explain then try to connect up
with anybody but myself sometimes it feels like I'm blowing out my
brains when I try to connect with her
who reminds me so much of the other her

My Business

I changed and you didn't like it
you didn't like it one bit
I changed
you couldn't control me
this time
you couldn't make me sit
down
under you
so you could be bigger
sit down under
so you wouldn't have to be the sitter this time
it's tough luck
and not my business really
your struggles aren't mine to contain
trying to make me smaller than you
really just keeps you lame
write me out of the script
in which you are afraid to play your
untamed part
out of control
so you have to control
by closing off me and your heart
I'm sorry that you hurt from before
and sorrier that I carried it for you
but I'm not sorry to feel strong now
and spontaneous
my feelings are not extraneous
they are real and will not be tucked away
for your comfort and illusion of control
I am alive with breath and the unexpected
I must let them together roll
out like a mat that welcomes this gait
that welcomes my budding change
if I must make a choice
I will
I'll leave you for my expanded range

Turning Pages

It was so confusing to be told
I was a happy child
and that I was lucky to have what they didn't have
I was happy
yes
my blood and bones were new
and happiness was an easy thing to carry through
but I knew
that they were hurting and
my happy childhood was always flirting
back to theirs
and forth to mine
back to their unconscious signs that like a storyteller
turning pages
twenty-four hours a day
I could read each word in everything they did
and with my happy
happy paid
and with my happy
happy laid down with them
happy was born to mend the invisible fence
I climbed it again and again
but how can you climb an invisible thing?
how can you know where to step or reach?
I was happy unwittingly
dragging their boat back and again to beach
and it always returned to the waves
happy comes and happy staves off the refuse in the water
happy clings to the fence and falls off into the water
and gets slapped by the unwieldy wet
is this a happy childhood bet?

It was so confusing to be compared
to be held up
to be snared
I know living things need to be reflected
it's too damn bad they were dejected
if I am going to be their rendering

I wish they could have cleaned their paintbrush a little better
I wish they could have knit a brand new sweater for me
as, for them, I sat
chilled
in their seascape
and hung on to their fence
smell narcissus in the air?
all right
I know children have to come from somewhere
and they also have to go
whose childhood, then, am I to tow?
hers?
where she was nearly aborted
on purpose
and I was planned
on which of those realities might I land?
it's interesting that although I was planned
she couldn't eat
when she was pregnant with a planned child
having it was quite the feat
could she relate to a planned child—to me?
I was almost aborted too
because her doctor said starvation just wouldn't do
and if her appetite didn't return I would have to be ejected
the next day he found her eating a lamb chop
a lamb chop was my happy childhood model
was I not hers to throttle?
and every time my happy brought smiles and
complimentary showerings
a giant towel was towering
to dry me off
and squeeze me hard so I could cough up every
happy I could muster
every happy in the cluster of unhappy was better than nothing
I suppose
was that a happy childhood rose to smell?
oh well

happy comes and happy goes
his, hers, theirs which of those?
I see now how my childhood grows into adulthood
I don't dare be too happy these days
I'm too afraid
I'm still in that phase
that hasn't as yet been introduced
to the happy
pure happy
my happy was induced
by a lack of happy

It was so confusing to be one of two
and to be the one that would do
all that couldn't be done in the past
it was confusing to watch the other one of two
be the mirror for the bitter blue
happy was very difficult
then
happy was sitting up in my pen
where I watched the other one of two
my sister
wear the family's blatant blister
emotional illness was her trouble
how else could she carry the family rubble?
how else could she construe the bitter blue?
the bitter undigested grief
welling up in her eyes
and dropping her jaw
and flailing her arms
it was so confusing to be happy
then

How It Works

This is how it works
she tells me I'm reliable
and then she leaves me alone
she leaves me alone
I am eight
she leaves me alone with my sister
with my kicking, screaming, writhing, tantruming, seizuring
older sister
she is ten
I am eight
I am eight
I don't want to be alone
I don't want to be with my sister
I am afraid of my sister
I am afraid of my mother all right I'll do it
I'll take care of her
I will be with her
I will be with her alone
I will be with her until the ambulance comes
I will be with her
and her seizure
and her buck teeth
and her mania
and her made fun of
in public
out in public
I will apologize for her
I will say she didn't mean to
she didn't mean to mean what she does
what she does is she is my mother
is mean
my mother mean
my mother means to say
she can't handle it
she wants me to
handle it
do it

take care of her
take care of her emotional illness
whose emotional illness
carries my mother
carry my mother's
my mother's package
my mother's in a package
a ten year old package
my sister
I'll do it
I'll be reliable
You can count on me to be
afraid
I am afraid
I am forty years old
afraid of reliable
because I remember reliable
with my sister

she is crying
my sister is crying
my father is hitting her
she yelled
she expressed anger
she went running
my father chased her into a room
slammed the door behind him
I was behind him
out
in the hallway
covering my ears
heard her screaming
what happening in there?
I am scared
what doing to her?
I will never do that
I will never do what my sister did
I will be good

I will be the best girl they ever had
I will clam up
jam up
best up
I will be a mute girl that's good
I am forty
I am good
I am afraid to say what I feel
especially when I'm angry and hurt

This is how it works
she tells me I'm responsible
she can count on me
she can count me in
to her dungeon to her monster movie no make-up Saturdays
climb into bed with her
ding-dong
get the door
she is hiding
we pretend
we pretend she is not hiding
she has a headache
get the door and make whoever it is go away
I lay
with her
she is warm
she is gentle
she feels ugly
gentle gets ugly
gentle is ugly
gentle is hiding
gentle is going
away
with her make-up
make-on gentle off
on the warpath
slash the ugly
don the mask don the raucous don the two-headed

dress-up
ignore me
dress down
implore me
to pretend along
two heads are better than one
no give me one
give me the one
give me the last
don't last
no time to pretend for her anymore any now I need gentle
to be beautiful
instead of ugly in her bed
on Saturdays

This is how it works
my father sees me
my father attends to me
my father adores me
my father—
she doesn't like that
my mother
my mother doesn't want that
she wants that
for herself
her father ignored her
and tended to her sister
her father criticized her
and adored her older sister
it isn't fair
it's her turn to be the one to be admired
but her daughter is
I am admired
I am her sister
the favored one
I play her sister
the one she wants to cast off
her sister and her daughter

cancel one out live through the other
which one should I be?
if he loves me, his daughter, she's happy she's sort of
his daughter
if I'm her sister and he loves me I'm in trouble
I see it in her eyes
in her resistance, in her anger
I can't compete with my mother, with my life-line
I can't compete with myself
her sister
his daughter
she can't live through me
but she lives through with me
if she wants me to stay because I have
and go away because I have
I can't have and have her at the same time
if I am loved
I lose my life-line
I'd better not be loved
I need love I need her I need my father
which way do I go to live?
which place do I go for love?
if one breathes the other suffocates
this is how it works
sweet and sour
go together
sweet and sour
sweet and sour
this is how it works
this is how but now I chose
to be faithful because
what I have known has kept me in the dark
and what I want to know now is the unfamiliar bright
faith is how it works to erase the memory
of night
faith is how I trust to get me past the fright
boasting to know better

this is how it works
that *can't* be how it works today
I want to be today
I want today to be
come the new familiar
today I want to say how I feel
today I want to be loved and not have to conceal
what I need
I need courage

Naked And Dressed

I am not the person I know myself to be
I am stronger and more secure
it's a different person that breathes inside of me
her reach is longer and knows for sure
that *this* strong brings not a burden
and is waiting to be retrieved
this strong can see the light of day
on the path that's yet to be conceived

I am not the person I knew myself to be
I am the person I am getting to know
and in the knowing
I become the unknown
in the unknown I am free
to be strong with room for a new memory
no pre-formed thoughts
or second guesses
strong without past association
a strong that neither hides out nor confesses
I can be strong and I can be solid for myself
now
without someone leaning into my heels
I can be strong without being abandoned
now
I'm just learning how that one feels
I can be strong without everything going wrong around me
I can be strong without all that commotion
I can be strong
I need to
to feel joy
true joy
that merits my equal devotion
I can be strong to be what I am becoming
in the shadow
I am blessed
I am naked on the moon
in the crescent
I am dressed

Spitting Image

*Cultural Incest in the Face
of a Nearly Forgotten Teenager*

Laid Out

I grew up in a china shop
where things were laid out
all glamorous
and light reflected from way up on top
the atmosphere seemed quite amorous
the china shop was my main world
impossible to replace
that is what I was told as a girl
in so many words to my face
I couldn't run in the china shop
or skip with joyful glee
the china shop had rules
that left a big impression on me
if something breaks
it'll be all over
if something breaks
I'll be blamed
if something breaks
I'll be banished
and won't that be a shame
if something breaks
it's not breakable
it's just that I did what shouldn't have been done
I should have been more careful
instead of having all that fun

Emblem

I don't want to tell what happened to me
I don't want to admit it
I am ashamed
I am embarrassed
I can never tell

I don't want to sound the bell
about what happened to me
and I want to ring it with all my might
how can I be mute with so much to say?
with so much to see and no sight?

they'll say, "don't look at the past—
stop analyzing—
think of today"
and I do
every time I look in the mirror *today*
I see my fifteenth year *today*
my last year
to have the face with which I was born
every time I look in the mirror
I see her plan to rip off what had begged to be torn

but I was not the beggar
I never begged for *that*
I begged only for acceptance
I know it
only for acceptance
most of all I wanted my mother to love me

so I set out
under foot—her above me
on a journey through her own personal desert
through this desert
she led me
it was there I was taught about unquenchable thirst
it was there I learned that I could drink
if I let *her* drink first
it was there I learned *how* to drink

the drink of the desert walker's curse—
futility filled her mammoth glass
she drank it hard and swallowed it fast
I watched her gulping it down her cavernous mouth
of that she had made a practice
since way before I came
by then she was eager to show off her cactus
and help me cultivate the same

she showed it to me inch by inch
I studied and memorized its strange fruit
as I grew into a fine imitation of it
I became irrevocably entwined in its root
and this root stretched across my mother's desert
like well-worn tracks for walking
step-by-step I walked like her
I watched her
drinking and stalking
and so I followed along the lines
bending to each rule
learning the lessons
false though they may have been
I got A's in my desert school
I wanted so to please my desert master
I wanted her to accept me
and even though her lessons weren't true
I practiced them adeptly

so I did as I was assigned
whatever she learned I would learn too
I let her teaching burn right through
to the other side of my soul
until I screamed out after I tripped
into the blaringly cavernous hole
this is the part where my desert guide's plan back-fired
it back-fired in *my* face
by pulling the root so tight around me
my fall devastated the place

you see, in this vast desert
she never spoke of her great thirst
she never mentioned her need to drink freely
she never let that fact speak first
so in this desert where I preened my cactus
and tripped over its prickly leaves
my blood spelled out across the sand
"we desert walkers are thirsty and bereaved!"
she didn't want to hear this
she didn't want to see
she never wanted to take that extra step around her pain
reflected in me

and now for the part I must tell
the part unbearably lame
but I was an obedient student then
taking in whatever came
now for the part that I must tell
the specifics of her back-fired truth
the part where premonitory wisdom was etched
into my arid youth
the part where the biggest step to pass
made me trip into the big, bitter morass
the part where all the desert walking
turned into vultures descending
the part where all her coaching and talking
turned into desperate unbearable squawking
the part where I did just like my mother did
and just like my mother ordered for me—twice
and just like a student who would never even think to oppose
I *let* her break and re-construct my nose
it was then that the map took an unexpected turn
when my soul took flight
from this gruesome sight
and left my body there to burn
left my body
there to act out the tragedy
as her beast turned inside out

the beast of thirst
the jammer
the beast of stuffed grief
stifled clamor
and total self-cessation
the beast that forged a facial feature
the beast of resignation

The tragedy is not that we lost the beautiful shape
of our own god-given proboscis
or that we had to go under the knife and hammer
but that we had to stifle the clamor
to take us as we are
she couldn't say, "take me as I am!"
then
I couldn't say, "take me or be damned!"
then
for she was already damned
and I was in her charge

so I wore my nose like an emblem
high above my heart
it stayed intact while the rest of me got brutally torn apart
and when I winced because it continually bruised me
to wear the beast like a glove
she couldn't bear the sight of herself
in the grip of conditional love

Today when I look in the mirror
I see my mother's *stunning* legacy
and I see me *honoring* my mother
and I see an unconscious decision
to *live*
I see it in my fifteen-year old face
I see what no lesson or ignorant rule
can ever even begin to erase
and I see my fifteen-year old
flunking out
breaking the rules

her innocence chased
I see her spirit's tomb
I see me beginning to find the path
adjoining me to *her* gloom
and I see me telling, asking, begging her
to come back to me
here
soon

She Begins To Speak

I wear my Chai today
I wear my full lips
and almond eyes
I wear my dark hair
wavy and thick
I wear my ears
and olive skin
I wear my candle with its clipped wick
I wear my nose
now thin
once thick
I smell myself sickened and sick of wearing the face
of involuntary sin
the casualty of separation from who I was born to be
the cataclysmic reverberation
worn
for all to see
and remember

She Continues

Like a rock that forms
from volcanic eruption
my face formed
through the years
every inch
every pore
every angle
a door
now locked in the middle of me
and crushed

Denial's Comeuppance

Noses are funny
not sad
most people say
not bad
not as bad as *real* life
not as bad as losing a life
not as bad as real shackles
not as bad as being real sick
not as bad as having to kick a drug or being in prison
be glad you didn't starve to death
or have to make a life-threatening decision

be glad
be glad
not so bad
not too bad
not that bad
not bad as bad

bad is not the point
and yes I did lose a life
not all but some
and any is worth grieving over
and yes I had on real shackles
because I had no choice
and yes I was real sick
having drunk the poisonous batter
and yes plastic surgery is a drug to be kicked
and yes starvation is the matter
the cover-up or alteration
cannot keep real problems hidden
real problems and real bad
grows out of things forbidden
grows out of what is not so bad
grows out of what is funny not sad
grows out of pointing a finger
the slightest bad unrecognized invites real bad to linger

Split Loyalties

Line up
line up
whose side are you on?
the truth is in your heart
your heart is at the bottom of the pool
filled with torn-aparts
the parts are scattered over there
just beyond your reach
your reach is bent by refracting light
the light is doused in dripping fright
the fright is contained from head to toe
your toes are pointing away to go
a way to go
where you don't know
that they don't care for your own soul
is trapped in sheer illusion
your body hides the trap
the mental lock jams with confusion

line up
line up
with your own life
first you must locate it
and just as you do
someone will come
and tell you that they hate it
they hate it from the other side
from there they'll try to bait it
from there they'll try to bring you aboard
just as you step out for air
they'll try to pull you back in
to suffocate with them in there
in there where they are on one side
the side that excludes the part
the side that says yes to the slave
and no to the trembling heart

line up
line up
whose side are you on?
put them all together
together as your sturdy boat
stands up to stormy weather

line up
line up
you get a call
a voice on the other end
tries to take your lined-up side
tries to make it bend
back to where fragments are dancing
prancing down the hall
back to where whips are cracking
back to where the fear is hacking
back to where dismembered hearts are stacked
and still stacking
pick up yours
and bring yourself
bring all your parts in packing

line up
line up
which side's deprived?
and which is never lacking?
line up
line up
one side's real love
the other is attacking
and who's attacking?
your own family
scrambling
mangling
you know
you know the voices
and the choice is

away from them you must go
but it is so very tempting
to line up on their side
even though your fragments know
that that's the side that made you go
into the pool of pieces
that's the side that says no to you
and yes to the book of Jesus
and yes to the rules all written up
and no to the insides written
no to the side where prophets live
yes to the lips in service did
spell out with words not deeds
for deeds come from the inside first
the side their own parts fled
line up, line up and say good-bye
to the other side instead
instead of saying yes to them
that say no to your heart
say no, yourself, to them
say yes to your lost parts

Wish

Listen with your child ears
not your parent trap
feel with your open heart
not your gaping gap
see with your outstretched hands
not the under-thumb demands
be at your ease
not your need to please
know of your selves
captured and sustained
sing them off the shelves
enraptured and re-claimed

My Fifteen Year Old's Return Introduction

I was banished to the skies
to the empty in my eyes
to the one without a home
to the twenty-five year old roam
I did vanish
bet my life
not her husband's or his wife's
I did vanish
with my life
with my life
hanging out there in the void
no one noticed
I had gone
not even me
I wafted back
surprise
with my anger on his table
never spoken
now she's able
I came to tell
of this
no fable
I came to tell
her first
now those
I came to smell an honest rose
I came to feel
I came, I chose
in the softness of her clothes
we fit together

Backtalk

Who am I talking to when I talk to you
and who's doing the talking?
did I conjure your resistance?
who am I walking with when I walk with you
and why do I walk with such insistence?
listen to what I'm saying
I might ask you to repeat it
it's my own form of praying
to hope you don't defeat it
when I say be whole
please
be whole
be whole and be complete
did you hear me
was that clear?
be whole now
and hurry
did you hear me?
can you hear?
I need the light behind your mirror

Conscious Aspirations

I've had enough growth for the week
for the month
for the year
forever
I want to be all the way grown
I want to know everything possible there is to know
and has ever been known
I want to have it all sewn up
I want to have control
I want to have an indestructible connection to my gelatinous
elusive soul
I want to stop getting sick or tired
I want to have boundless energy
I want to celebrate life
is that a crime?
I want to be unconscious of time
I want to cure this cold
I want to never grow old
I want my eight year old body back
I want to never be told by the voice that plays inside my head
at the slightest provocation
The voice that looks my situation over
and offers that tried and true summation—
it's not gonna work
so give up and fear
it's all a game inside of here
and outside is not much better
so curl up into a ball and take your fall
and do not jostle that permanent fetter—
OK, never mind
give me growth
give me endless mystery
give me all those corners around which my naked eye can't see
give me trust in something bigger
something to which I am connected
give me the must in the *I can't*s or *shouldn't*s
give me the will in the *might I*'s or *wouldn't*s

give me that ever-loving mammoth body of unknowns
I can't think of anything better to be subjected to
anything less than life-threatening
would be taking the easy way out
and life is hard
we all know that
life is playing that face-down card
life is struggle
life is change
life discussed in so many words makes me feel deranged
so let me spin it like a record
and let the notes play without a visible conductor
and let me hear the song I've yet to hear
and when the notes go winding around that cliff so steep
give me something to hold onto
when I let go
something to keep
something in me
preserved not pickled
something loyal amidst the fickle
something warm and something sure
is that possible?
just that
just pure
just something little, tiny, an inkling
so I can face the dark
something to take with me when I pull up stakes
when I take it out of park
something that holds me like a cup
contained and open with a handle
something to keep me together
while something else gets dismantled
something that moves me with pleasant surprise
within a new frame and structure
something that reaches beyond my current grasp
something that links it all together with a clasp
of a somewhat recognizable design

something that belongs to everybody
in different ways
including my own way
and mine

Hand-me-down

In the year of the flower
an inch above ground
I saw the wind capture my sister
In the smear of the hour
I heard bevelled sound
the wind became a twister
in the space between her legs
mine I don't remember
in the space between her legs
her April turned to December
in the space between her legs
she was horrified
and loud
she felt vilified
no crowd came to sing the welcome tune
just shame
no celebratory moon
we in the suburbs drew no mesh of poetic lines
for the timely fluids that flow without consent
we in the suburbs drove to drugstores instead
quietly purchasing sundry items for female consumption
funless packs of invisible tacks
that post the small bodily defeats
all over your mind
it was a defeat for my sister dear
the week-end we stayed with my aunt and uncle
parents out of town
they missed her haunting frown
and her body crashing down
and the mayhem
I didn't—no
I didn't miss a lick
no
I saw it all
and I remember her frantic call
asking nature to please stop coming
her pain was like a gnarly drumming

deep inside my head
protrusions of the dread taking root there
in preparation for my flowering stint
no separation from my sister's indelible imprint
only my own
what did *I* have to look forward to
when my body took its turn?
when it did
what kind of salve could I mix for it—
madness or amnesia?
I picked the latter
today I can't remember my very own first
probably quiet
splatter
so quiet to be echo-less
the space between my legs
I can't remember the space between my legs
for her screaming

Appeal To A Former Self

Tell me your tale
little girl of before
I really want to know it
even though my habits of recent and past time do not show it
am I safe enough for you now?
I won't tell you what to do now
you tell me
what is the truth of your days gone by?
when you stood inside yourself
when your arms and legs were your own
when your hands were too small to pick up a phone and say—
please come help me I am trapped!
what did you see with those eyes
then?
what awesome horror became uncapped?
was it your sister falling apart?
tipping things out of control?
your mother—
forcing you to play the caretaker role?
your father clinging too tight?
your father and sister in their tumultuous engaging?
or any one of those three taking their turn raging?
and leaving you all alone?
did something happen in the void of your abandonment?
something crucial?
something obscene?
I can barely remember you
much less what or where you might have been
that scared you right out of your body
now mine feels like a zillion triggers
on the verge of going off
which look?
which scenario?
which mundane act will detonate the next pivotal memory?
if you tell me your tale
I'll turn to greet it
and feel you at long last

sharing my skin
I can feel your panic
and your fear of scrutiny
and your exuberant body's love of spring
I want to remember what you knew in detail
I want to join you in everything
please trust me

Voluntary Plea

I ask the child for forgiveness
don't *you* ask the child to forgive[2]
because *I* have been resistant to learn
and *my* attention slow to turn
to face her face straight on

I ask the child for forgiveness
and more patience
which she has had for years
waiting for me to see her
blinded by my fears
which I *learned* to have from early on
I learned how not to trust her
I learned how to ignore her
and think I couldn't afford her
did everything to ward her off
and out
in time
I learned the routine as though it were mine
ignorant of the fact that it is *she* who is mine
not the multi-generational dance I do
drunk with inertia through and through
taking seldom the chance to meet her
and acquaint myself
so sweet her
constant quest to survive
she is quintessentially alive in me
I ask her to please help me be
with her
more often
and peel away this coffin
within which I laid her down to sleep
with a watchful eye upon *me*
never forceful
never coercive
just there
constant her loving stare—

waiting for me to share with her my breath
she asks for so little
and I so much

forgive me, little girl
I'm still building in me a world
where we can live together

Gapped

Stuff, stuff, stuff, stuff,
stuff, stuff, stuff—
broccoli, carrots, sweet potatoes
gobs
they're healthy
I'm wealthy with organic vegetarian food inside
but it puts me into a mood, a trance
I wish I could take the chance
to be an empty stomach for once
what could fill it up
if I left it empty?
fear, anxiety, doubt, piety—
the looming empty space
like a jaw lunging at my face
I gnaw on those vegetables, fruit and grain
like there's no tomorrow
and like there's no today
because full mouths can't play spontaneously
within this feed-me structure
I have repeatedly dared to rupture my delicate appetite
for the ethereal dish
cracked as I sit on top of it
eating another concrete meal
"hey! what's the deal?
people are starving in other places
how can you complain about having the choice to refuse
your food of choice?"
my starvation needs a voice too
hunger comes in many forms
let's not put the brakes on the ones that don't conform
to a linear frame of mind
my hunger is the kind that can't be satisfied with money
or staved off with sugar or honey
my hunger is the elusive rind
I'd suck it if I could only find
the fruit around which it is wrapped
I'd bite it but my teeth are proverbially gapped

and there is no corner store to shop in
no take out to call up or drop in
no list to check off at the end of the week
I'd like to fill my cheeks that easily
I'd like to put a request in some obviously accessible place
I'd like to have my hunger understood
to be so literal to be suspicion-free
you can't see, touch or hear what's really missing in me
so I can't explain it
but believe me
I am hungry

Just Itself

Can I find a place
out
in the community
if I believe I don't deserve it?
if I've been taught the world won't swerve to fit my direction
because of how I look?
because of how I don't look
look
I'll never look the way I was *taught*
my appearance will never obey what ought to be the way to look
my appearance will never sway in step with the end-all-be-all
book of rules

From the time I was a teenager
for at least three years
I received annual subscriptions to seventeen magazine
for a present
pictures of blonds
from sun up and on
invaded my head
and told me it's their look instead
that has the right to live
give, give, give your impressionable self over
or was it my self they took over
my self they crooked over

If your historical image was cooked over the coals
if your ethnic appearance was a life or death situation
which mine was
I suppose you ought to change it
for life
but what kind of life was mine to have
when my worth was measured by a non-intuitive eye?
an eye on exteriors
a subliminal—you must comply because you are inferior
because worth was
still is
a comparative thing

instead of just itself

Can I make a place for myself in the community
a place from which to contribute something of my self
something valuable
when my value was reduced down to outside appearances?
no sixth sense adherences were ever mentioned
to be a valuable way
to be
a valuable, stable seed upon which to build and grow
and show
out
in the community

Can I show myself out in the community
can I receive reception out in the community
can I manifest a kind mirror
out
in the community?
when what I have
in here
is what I have to give
and what I learned about myself was
I have little right to live
much less give
because of how I look
and I have a good memory

The Oldest Scapegoat On Earth

Yes
it is possible
to be seduced
by a parent
parent to child
mother to daughter
and she did
with her humor
her fire
and my dire need to feed my feeder
yes
but now I must weed her out of my garden
because I have learned to feed myself
and seize the tilth by my own hand
my earth
my earth
commands me to stand up for myself
not in the shadow of anyone's denial
stand up
spread the wealth
in even proportion
no warped-out contortion need fill my shoes
or clothes or hat
none of that bouncing invisible ball
I don't have to catch your heavy, hidden thoughts at all
or wear them
so you can pare them down to a comfortable size
I can read your eyes
don't be surprised when I lead this conversation into a hole
we're in it together
my expression did not put us there
it merely made our being there more obvious
and that's exactly where seduction always gets me
into a hole
I forget and remember the threat
of being in a dependent body
Oh god she

does it to me time and time again
in a plethora of forms
and I let it happen
again and again
because I forget and remember when
I danced for the big people
took no chance with the big people
but romance with the big people was delicious
everything was delicious when I was small
I didn't differentiate at all
because life came at me in every which way
which way was right
which way was wrong
I was in love with the throng of pulsations
and I went for that and this and those
my tingling toes took me everywhere and anywhere
and all of it
alive
I didn't know how seducingly contrived it all was
and the call was
to be their servant clown
did I read the job description before I came down
to this flesh trap?
yip, yip, yap
I barked—they clapped
I cartwheeled—they sapped their tragic, magic mirror on two legs
and said, "go! get out of here!"
when I looked the most like what they hated
was I fated to be their reflective pool?
what tapering, mimic school did *I* swim in?
sometimes I wish I could row to an inside-out island
where everybody knows what they're about
from the inside out
I have no doubt
in that place
I would be my own clown
dancing 'round to the rhythm of my own sound

but we are an interdependent society
or we are heading
should I say hearting on that way
and when we get there
what will happen when we look in each other's eyes—
who will cry out with the varied, buried cries?
on the inside-out island no cries are buried
because everybody cries
and sings
for now
I will
but not by seduction
I'll try conscious deduction
and make my choice
I only hope that my motion
moves forward the notion
of you
and me
we too

Overdue Platform

I heard a man's voice on public radio
an author of a book
his interviewer spoke plainly
about this man's cognitive behavioral approach to life
and said to this man, "Look,
I know people who express anger
get it out and feel much better afterward!"
The man said, "For how long?"
and
"Oh yes, it's fine for the moment
but it comes back
the anger always comes back—
my book has some mindful steps to take
a list, a way to avoid mistakes
think—
instead of blowing off steam
think—
join the thinking team!"

I didn't think anything
I had no cognitive experience at all when I heard this man speak
I felt
I felt
I felt my anger peak
at the foot of this man's frozen mountain
this behavior-preaching geek
this author
this expert
this mental body advocate
I wanted to scream—
who is going to speak up for the emotional body for once?
"hoodlums" in LA?
who is going to speak out for the emotional body
what next dunce is going to tell it to go away?
with their published words in black and white
radio voices, magazines, TV shows
who in the media will pick up the emotional plight

and stop telling its body to go?!

if I hear one more "approach"
one more "public safety recommendation"
police chief and mayor
"organizing" to hold down the fort
go ahead—hold it down
and then watch your ordered underlings contort
and explode
that's what happens when you hold it down
explode or implode
pick your poison
this is war
the mental body and emotional sore

why is it that the mind can carry on unscathed
it can think and think away?
it can tinker and tamper
and never be hampered
and force the heart to pay
the heart—the emotional body
never forces its hand like that
I wish the heart could be so pat
but it's not
and that's the rub
that's the unappetizing grub
that few people are willing to hunker down and swallow
the real mistake is thinking that the emotional body lives
only to make you wallow in it
that is wrong!
the emotional body is playing a magnificent song
with three lyrics that say
I am alive!
I am alive!
I am alive!
please join the chorus
and maybe the mental and emotional body
will stop being a mutual abhorrence

and start dancing together
without stepping on each other's toes
the heart and head must deep down know
that they were made to live together in an *un*conceivable perfect peace
if the heart and head would move in together
I believe sickness, war and violence
would relinquish their soul-forsaking lease

Pull Up

I cannot tolerate a lie
an emotional lie
I cannot withstand it
I cannot endure
a pleated tongue
and make-nice demure
I cannot listen to one more excuse
a "busy, busy life"
and message machine refuse
don't tell me you're busy
tell me you have unconscious priorities
because that's the reason that you made plans
and then cancelled them at the last minute
your priorities knew the score right from the start
and I knew too
but I couldn't find it in my heart to protect myself from you
I got caught up in the fold of your subtle condescension
your pleated tongue never mentioned
you had no original intention to meet me on this day
but something greeted me to say—
when she made her excuse
why did I feel so reduced?
and I felt that from the start
because your excuse came then
when you said
we needed one to meet
you said, "this will give us an excuse…"
you said it to be *sweet*
why didn't *I* say then—
I can mail you your book back
we don't have to meet
excuses are no way to pull a seat to the table
I am able to say
no!
to this spread of guilt
no one said you have to see me
no one said you had to feed me an obligatory meal

or lend me your book
or cut me a deal
except maybe you
why is there disarming cordiality in everything you do
and why am I so receptive to it?
and who are you acting like?
and who do you want me to play?
your needy-self-daughter to a father who's always away?
and making nice about it
and making you crazy
he must have made you crazy
with his good father full of promises facade
dumping out his hateful manipulative wad of candy-coated guilt
it's all over me now
from you
I should have noticed how this trap got built for two
right from the beginning
why am I always winning this hardship role?
I want to stop paying this bridge to friendship toll
and build the bridge to myself
stronger
take more time even if it takes a lot longer
to stop acting out the pain of an unconscious brain
and learn how to sustain emotional honesty
with a capital H
two poles connected in the middle
in the middle of me
not me to you
because if I direct my needs
to the kind of friend that pretends to be one
but continually shuns contact
or lends it that baiting air
then when I cross *that* bridge
I'll probably fall off into yesterday's water
where my stance could get no tauter
as the believing little daughter
that bought my parents act too

the act of never-mind-the-contradiction-between-what-we-say-
and-do
now I'm big enough to not budge from what I feel as true
right from the beginning
it was then I knew
I didn't really need to meet with you at all
to play up to that act
that call
that set-up
must become a dead priority

these days
I better make it a conscious priority
to birth new ways
unearth the maze to myself
first
make plans with myself
first
be a friend to myself
first
listen to myself
first
especially when she knows better

As Inside So Outside

Can you look at this?
I don't want to
I can't
can you look at this
of mine
and tell me it's good—
tell me it deserves recognition
and that it could
do for others
what for me it did?
tell me
then, I'll tell my kid
my kid inside who was told not to look
and that others' looking was more important
and that I should see what in their eyes is going on with me
and how I shouldn't know
in their eyes
I was not to be
because their eyes had ceased to see their own *kid*
can you tell me
I don't have to do what they did?

Can you look at the work I've done
and know that it's made of the same stuff as the rising sun?
can you tell me that all my hours of concentration
and honorable intention
deserves, at least, an honorable mention
and maybe even first prize
can the honor match the size of my diligent efforts?

Can you tell me I'm like all the others
and that I am also unique
can you tell me that I can mix the two—
I can belong to me and fit in with you?
you
you tell me
because I need to know
and I have a very difficult time telling myself it's so

hard
to listen in there
and bend to that way
if you tell me first then maybe I can learn to say—
yes!
I am imbued with everything going on inside me
that's true, real, valuable
inside
and then I look around and hear not one sound that confirms this
I stand by a bus
inhale the gust
that tells me to stop breathing
or at least to stop noticing that my air is gone
and nobody else is blocking the stench
they look at me like I should
time-out on the bench
and keep my beauty lost and tucked away
and offer up my very life
as though it were made to defray the cost of negation's travels
can you summon a witness with your gavel
and have the witness watch you tell everybody
to tell themselves that they are good, right, worthwhile
and breathable
and that it's not a question of conflicting styles
but a question with the wrong reply?
all those that told me my insides lie
in so many moving shapes and forms
safety in numbers
safety in norms
the safety to which my little one had to conform
safety for years
the status quo
the safety of every audible and subliminal voice saying
no!
no wonder it's so hard to listen to this in me
and unabashedly know that I deserve a better mirror
outside reflections of inside here

and if inside just happens to be
beautiful and harmonious and free
and I know it for sure
you won't have to tell me another thing about it
because my whole world will shout it
automatically

But first
of course
I'll have to pass through some channels
lots of static
and more resistance
until I am shaken out of this deceptive complacency
with more insistence
so that I will look at all that I have created
and know that it is good
and know I must drop the encroaching hood
and admit myself
in earnest
exposed as self-seen
disconnecting the internal and external
negation machine

Relative Points

I was incested in a stationery store
I was
I was incested there
I was innocent and unsuspecting
a victim
forced to bear
the ill-fate of a brutal attack
from the side
not the back
it happened when I dropped my pack of merchandise
I heard a voice coming at me
coming for me
aiming to break me down
an incestor to be sure
sure and bound
to impose herself and then pretend it didn't happen
but it did
what's more
it hurt
to hear my attacker blurt
with a stifler's air in a helper's disguise
she laid her eyes on my items on the floor and said
"Oh! You're not doing too good!"
and
"Did you break it?"
I dropped my stuff and she said
the very instant it crashed down
"You're not doing good!"
who asked her opinion to come 'round
and slam itself upon my day
my day
because I dropped a few things?
I'm supposed to pay
by surrendering my own sense of what just happened
to her attack
and be grateful for it
and maybe even offer back

a thank you
for doting
when, in fact, she was goading me to feel like shit
for having dropped it
but did I lose by dropping?
did I chose to place my items on a tippy surface?
which I mistook as stable
I mis-took
I took the surface for something able
for something other than what it was
and then I learned in no uncertain terms
what a tippy surface does
it drops my things on the floor
no less
no more
it doesn't decide that I'm not doing too good
I'm doing great
I'm taking my lessons as part of my fate
that's doing good
I think
I'm allowed to make mistakes aren't I?
to have my things drop
I'm allowed to have them fall
I'm allowed to have my process
mis-takes and all
without thinking I'm doing badly
and I'm allowed to reject what was trying to make me feel sad-ly
but I couldn't prevent it from coming
I couldn't foretell her imposing her hell
and cut-no-slack perception
I couldn't prevent her from foisting on me
her low-grade self-reflection
but I could and did tell her
"*I'm* doing fine—
I just dropped something—
and no it didn't break."
and my oh my but you're a fake
I didn't say that but I thought it and I thought

her words were not helpful at all
although her intonation implied such
her incestuous words did give much
in the way of a very unwelcome touch

next time someone besides me
assesses *my* situation
and offers their explanation
as though it spelled out my reality like a spelling bee champ
I'll say that's not good spelling
that's a clamp
that's cultural incest
that's a rampant field
you don't need a license
you don't need a monetary yield to motivate you
you just need to externalize your every inner twist
and apply it to someone else's gist
and never miss
an opportunity to step in
step on
step over whoever you can
with a judge-mental mind
the truly insidious kind
that says, "I see better what you've seen"
before you even see it
cultural incest is very mean
it's like hitting with an invisible bat
how many times do we all do that?
it's a fine detail
I know
but the big picture is full of those
who dress in correct and neighborly clothes
ready to strip you down to their size
just hand them back their groping eyes
and see yourself
as clearly as you can permit
using uninvited come-ons
to focus your own wit

Put Down Your Pen

My sister was never mine
my sister
mine
mein sister
she belonged to the machine
and her place on the chain
turning the monster over
she belonged to the spit
impaled by it
embroiled
shoulder to shoulder

my sister was never mine
I've stopped trying to reach her
and the part of myself that sistered her
will never again beseech her
but my sister is there—
she has an address and I do too
and she writes letters
to the girl that she once knew
and insists upon speaking the old language
so her letters come in tangled tongue
and fill me with deep anguish

she tries to reconnect me to the machine
with pincers
so grotesque
she tries to nab my little girl clean from me
and instead she makes a mess

I wish my real sister could come out of hiding
or disengage the hold
of the predatory machine that keeps dividing
and keeps keeping things so cold
between us—
rocks and metal
once placed there
now forgotten but remaining
old thoughts, needs

now habits—
a calcified system sustaining
sustaining the machine
that's all
just the machine
not us
not sisters
not living spontaneous new loving beings
the machine
is what writes those letters to me
the machine is what I'm seeing
the machine forges her name
the machine made her insane
I never knew back then
when I protected my *sick* sister
I never knew I protected them
them! the machine that fixed her
the machine of vicious cycles
the machine of involution
which ones are pinions?
and which ones are free to activate their own revolution?
not my sister
not mine
my sister mine
mein sister

I wish she would stop pretending
I wish she would stop trying to reconnect me
every word of hers defending the machine
"Come join me," she says
"Come back to the machine!"
but I have disengaged myself
and re-engaged with something else
a massively different system
I can't communicate with words about it
because her machine ears will counter and twist them
she will decide that I'm selfish and defiant
not what I am—

respectfully self-reliant
she knows only the vicious machine ways
my sister is the machine
to it she devotes her dwindled days

so
I can't have her
she can never be mine
I can't sister the sister
I remember
I remember when I didn't know
that you were never mine
my sister
sister mein
belongs to the machine
why?!
to the machine
why?!
and how I cry
to the machine
to the machine
to the machine
I say good-bye

Hold Your Own Hand

There's a line here
I must cross it
I *have* crossed it
I have crossed it with one foot
I have crossed it with half my soul
I have climbed half way up the pole
I look back
I see people
friends
who have kept me company
on my way to the pole
on my way to the line
they escorted me there
we escorted each other
I thought
then they stopped
walking
it's my pole
my line
they're not coming with me so it must be mine
my crossing

I don't want to let go of their hands
the line is deep
my feelings are steep
I don't understand
why can't they come with me on this journey?
why does this split feel like they're turning
away?

If I stay on their side of the line
I disappear
no one seems to mind
it is clear that
this side of the line has no room for me
but I'm here
where am I when I'm here?
on this side of the line

on their side?
I nod
I keep people comfortable
I reassure them that the pole
the line
doesn't even exist
that on this side
there is nothing to be missed
but I know better
I know about the other side
the other
where there's room for me
and anyone else who chooses to be
there
there is light there
on the other side
light where
I can see myself
I don't have to hide
I don't have to hover
I can be sure, stable
a lover of me on my own terms
I can be here completely
but without the familiar others who came so far
only so far
will they join me later?
will they climb the pole?
will I meet others?
must I go alone?
until then?
until when?
how long?
how wide a crossing is it?
how high the pole?
if I say yes to myself
I must say no to the side of the line
where I can't go

where I can't be
where friends
family
people sit and refuse to see the pole at all

I hear its call
I hear them too
I can't know what to do
until I do it!
I can't have a guarantee
I really want to move it
fast and far
away but towards
away to afford myself some room
some air
it's so hard to bear
this split
this conversion
how can I be tempted at all
by that perversion?
that suffocating blanket to which I have clung
a corner
twisted but familiar by which I have hung
a mere fragment of myself
and I thought it was me
I thought
I thought it was me that hung free
But I didn't
I dangled there
on the end of the square
on their side of the line
and bent when the blanket folded
I cringed—
wasn't meant to be molded
but I *was* molded a certain way
and in order to go that way
I tucked in much of myself

so much to get frayed
and then the line reinforced my thread
the line taught me how to tread
and reach for the other side
the other seemingly horrific divide
but the divide
on one side is in the middle of me
and on the other side
the divide comes up through the we
the me and those
cozy in our
closed out together way
that never looks at the inclement weather
that never says it's an emotional storm
an emotional storm
in the eye of our hearts
where the storm is housed
where the division starts
I see the division that's when I aim for the pole
I see the division
and how it takes its toll
I see the division
I see the line
I see the division
it's not just mine
I see the division
like an electric blade
with a silent motor
in the sleepers' arcade
it whirs—
I won't notice if you won't notice
so we can keep the *family* together
I won't notice if you won't notice
this rope, that chain, our tether

So to cross the line is to remove the divide in me
and make a division between the we

we who were never really undivided in the first place
we were always divided in the worst way
in ourselves

So the line is really the bridge
the closer I get to myself
the further I am from the others
the others who won't go near their bridge
their line
their pole
I want those I love
have loved
have known
to go
to cross their bridge
to find the home
in them
so we can be together
when will they cross it?
when will *we* be?
I ask
I plead
I concede
I must head for the pole
I must head for me
no matter what

Teetering

Who am I kidding?
I'm out on this limb
with my outstretched self
with this clip and trim
scratching people off my list of investments
who am I kidding—
with my don't-write-me-'til-I-write-you behestments?
it's not a plan
it's a whim
who am I kidding?
I'm out on this limb
who am I kidding?
I've got to change my mind back
I haven't written my mother for it seems too long
and my sister I'm about to tell her to get gone
without a single explanation
how destructive it seems
this creation
to put myself out on this limb
away from what, who and with whom I've been
who am I kidding?
it can't last
who am I kidding?
I can't fly at half-mast
and feel unencumbered at the same time
for the first time I do
it's no joke
this limb is true
and really, really strange

who am I kidding?
I can't do this
I can't go it alone
will I even be missed really?
and who is it they'll miss in my absence
when my absence was part of the deal?
who will they miss
one more member on their wheel of defacements?

I'll thank them to find their own replacement for me
or whoever it was that they thought me to be
it's that one I am no more
it's that one who found the door to herself
and entered to find someone else—
her forgotten self
crouching and waiting
her forgotten self
dodging the grading
the rating
the berating
the stamp
the ramp to myself was fraught
how oh how I've fought to get to her
so broken and unsure of herself
I have seen her now
talked to her
been with the part of myself
that went far away
was driven away
driven out
told she could not live in me
told in no uncertain terms not to be
but she continued somewhere
someway
and now that we've been reunited
I can't allow us to be divided again
even though it might mean
permanent separation from certain people
thoughts
ways
beliefs
comfort zones
deferential days
certain habits
perspectives
attitudes

the residential maze
I don't want to live *there* anymore
because I want to live
I'm out on a limb
because I want to live my life
without the sieve
unmeshed
let me live
on my own behalf
let me give
I have real worth
and to know it
I must administer my own whole birth
practically all by myself
because when I look around
I see a conspiracy crashing down
it's saying, "abort yourself!" instead
I need this limb
I am out on this limb
to keep breathing

Spitting Image

How can I own my feelings
when I don't even own my face?
isn't that incredible?
I don't own my face
I don't own my face?!
how is this possible?
and what do my feelings have to do with my face?
highly improbable
for this connection to erase
one from the other
and why add them
why bother?

I will tell you
as I stand out on this limb
and I look down
it's very dim
I can barely make out
what is happening in me
that brings me to my face
my teeth
my nose
without them I am bare
and I am bare
because I am without them
outrageous!
even I contest
I have teeth
I have a nose
which one of those is troubling me now
and making me see nothing there
and no place where my feelings dare to be felt?

A long time ago
after I had grown
for so many years—
thirteen and fifteen to be exact
I was put up on the rack

because I had grown several inches too far
because the final spurt brought my teeth up slightly crooked
and my nose out too wide
too long
too contemptuously familiar
this had to change!
bring on the metal
the wires
the tools
the once or twice a week after school
for two years
the two trips to the surgeon
without tears
to make the appearance fit
the appropriate limit
'til I gag and spit the acceptable face
and be sure to chase
off
every one of my feelings about it
because this is a gift
my parents gave to me
this twisted and turned
pounded and chiseled
face
a gift
I must see
that gratitude is the only thing I should feel
they worked so hard to provide this yield
this
straightened teeth
this
straightened nose
the original ones were surely my foes
and the straightening was worth every penny
no matter the cost
the pain—
physical or psychic shame

"this is a gift"
"we are sure"
as if out of pure interest for my welfare

couldn't they see in my empty stare
how tortured I was?
how *gone* I was?!
and what this day in day out reconstruction does
to the heart of a teenager
split apart by the rearranger
that tells her with each manipulation—
who she is and who she ought to be are two very separate things
something here rings
a note rather sour
in the we-will-buy-you-a-proper-face-and-pay-by-the-hour-
because
your face—
your face—
because—
I really don't remember if or how they justified this
base and primitive treatment
of a girl who wanted only to be accepted from the start
but this was normal in *my* neighborhood
this face changing
this is what we do
the ones who did
the ones I knew
were each and every one of them a Jew

not to mention teenagers who were very conscientious of how they
looked
in those days
how you look and who you are are one and the same
so if you *can't* like how you look
you better change how you look
and how do you decide this?
do you decide it alone
or because you're scrutinized down to the bone?

I know *I* was
I know I didn't
couldn't
come to the table or leave the house
without making sure first
over and over
not a hair was out of place
if only I could have made sure that my face
was just so and right enough to be left alone
to grow just as how it pleased
but it didn't please
as though I were contagiously diseased
I would have been terribly teased
or so they logic'd
I would have been rejected too
without these operations
what in the world would I do?
so let's get the rejection over in calculated strokes
even if she gags and chokes
eventually we will spit the proper face
buy a kit and make a cure
remove the wrong face
for her

"for we are good parents,
good parents—
good providers"
I'd say they were effective dividers
teaching me how to keep my feelings separate
from what they truly were
teaching me how to keep those experiences
trapped in an emotional blur—
I had no idea that I was not grateful for their gift
that I was more
much more than miffed
I was crushed
literally and psychically

and only realized it twenty-five years later

all that activity
all that pain
all that money
all that pain
all that effort
all that pain
educated experts, expensive supplies
offices, hospitals
travel time
loving parents
carting me to the designated locations
pain, more pain
more consultations
pain
follow-up visits
raping my brain
every detail, every effort
convincing me
systematically
that I must need
I must need this
because there is something in me that is grossly amiss
something that is in desperate need of fixing
but no one ever really explained why
why it was all mixing together
and indistinguishable
how I felt about it all
was easily extinguishable
"we were lucky to have the money"
"lucky to have the choice"
how lucky could I have been to be
me without a voice?
and if they say now
I wanted it then
could abetting such acts be right?

years later I realized that I was paralyzed with fright
to not want it
and to say I, truly, did not want it was not an option at all
and would have been an unbearable threat
how could I accept myself as is
when those that raised me had not, themselves, as yet
one died before doing it
and the other
to this day is still eschewing it
and to this day I am not convinced
that whatever it was so terribly wrong with me was fixed

so here I am bare
without my features
a crafted recoiled creature
trying desperately to separate out my teachers
the ones to whom I give failing grades
for encouraging my deepest feelings to fade
but these feelings linger
these feelings wait
until I own them as my own along with my face
which one of those is in a retractable state?!
one beckons me to track it at last
more than twenty-five years after
the image was cast

The Little Engineer That Could

And so I did it without tears
I did it all without tears
and without an ounce of anger
I was the other daughter
I was the non-demander
dangling in suspended animation
while I watched my sister
dodge and dance damnation
I crouched off in a corner
hid my heart
disguised the mourner in me
and carried on ever so quietly
never daring to throw my hat in the ring
I wore it over my eyes
never looked at anything
inside
nor divulged my festering cries

for what could be the reason
to cry?
everything was all right
I was lucky
I had no call
compared to my parents
especially my mother
who "had the worst childhood of all"

so between my mother and sister
I didn't stand a chance
I was the talented one
and funny
I carried all the romance in life
adorable and loved
placed way up above
my sister and her
I was the happy one of the three
I was happy—that's me
what did *I* know about feelings or pain

my sister was sick
my mother ashamed
I was the last remaining ticket
I had better be as I should
I had better entertain the lot
especially the ticket purchaser
but good

but
what if
by chance
this two-legged romance
had reason
lots of reasons to feel other than bright?
what if
by chance
this whole arrangement
purporting to be day
was actually the darkest of night?

don't express it
I was told
but feelings inevitably unfold
in whatever way they can
I stored mine in a huge internal bin
until it boiled right to the edge
like a subterranean engineer
clever under there
in thirteen years I built myself a right and honorable ledge
call it a migraine
how convenient
guaranteed
to prompt a lenient response
from all those of pressing concern
it took thirteen years to build
this fine, outstanding ledge
I stood on it
so my feelings could take their turn

insuring this "happiest" child turned teenager
to have at long last with good reason
a special occasion
her very own season
when she could be literally blind
with hallucinations
regurgitations
overflowing her feelings to her own sweet heart's content
convincing
justifiable
and absolutely reliable
no questions as to where happy went
with her head imploding and body eroding
to bed I was immediately sent
in anger, fear, angst and confusion
my heart reeling
anger, fear, angst and confusion
no wonder she is feeling
anger, fear, angst and confusion
she is sick—
carte blanche
free expression
my road out of repression
at least as long as I was sick
I could have at it
crying and writhing
a clear shot
no denying
my protection for these unattractive scenes was thick

unlike my sister who outrightly revolted
and was correspondingly jolted
I set my whole package on automatic pilot
when I was well
I stuffed it
swallowed it and shoved it
when I was sick
I was *loved* for it

and comforted by dad
whose own secret sadness
was quelled by this madness
my condition
brought *his* dis-ease into temporary remission

Through the years my machine stood me in good stead
when a true feeling was prompted
no one else need tromp it
by now *I* knew how to drive myself to bed
for that automatic punishment
when impolite feelings stirred
I deported them all to my head
to blow up into a migraine
call it demon possession
how was I to know it was
chronic regression—
back to the familial fascist state
where *righteous* commandments continued to rule my fate
keeping me within my childhood's limits
where being mute was the strict order of the day
and feelings are confined to the involuntary grimace

Knowing this does not completely correct it
because this system connects
to my survival according to old rules
in order to change them and keep me from danger
I have to wake up in a brand new school
where I am head master
where I make the rules—
kindly and compassionately permitting my own heart
if my engineer built structures to block it
she can consciously take them apart

Welcome Home

What price a teenager
what price a child
what price her heart
pure and wild
what price to silence her natural reactions
to split her sensations into cold warring factions
what price to build her only to dock
what price to wire the bomb to her clock

count out in numbers
each essence
each beauty
lock up the sum in daughterly duty
forget about the vault and hide away the key
until the forgotten teenager comes back to haunt me

"I can't do it"
"I can't cope"
"I can't cover this task"
I can't remember the day I put on their mask
"I'm incompetent"
"I'm ashamed"
don't ask me to think clearly
it took twenty some years to remember that I nearly
sold my heart away for good
believed it when they said I should
stop feeling
exactly the way I did
shielded my own eyes as they covered me with their lid
what price I paid to nearly kill my own kid
for my parents
who short-changed my value
who underestimated my time
my feelings
my know-how
what is rightfully mine
they tagged it and closed it into a crypt
I carried it myself with no awareness of it

until the mummy awakened in her tightness
her box
too rigid, too small for her
with a plethora of locks
she burst it open with full feelings
on her incipient vine
current events forcing her to face them and climb
up and tall
recognition through the wall

she reaches for me
her arms unlatched
I open my heart
with it we catch each other

In Memory of Mute

Monologues in the Collective Mouth

Dedication

In memory of mute
I wave my hands and point to the buried frown
In memory of those
all those who recoiled when they were ordered to
shut up and sit down
In memory I cry
and cringe and boil
the stunted attempts
reprimanded or foiled
the hunted sips of raw emotion
shot straight back into murky oceans
In memory of the tear
the hairline crack
that spreads like wildfire down the middle of my back
every time I think of opening my mouth
In memory of doubt
mute's reinforcer
tripping up my path and making it coarser
In memory of fear
mute's escorter
the tireless crimp
the heart contorter
filling up my house with silent boarders
who never see the light of day
In memory of the muted way
of the selves
my selves I smothered
In memory of the me who became some other me
In memory of what I became
In memory of every trapped cell in my brain
confined in bitter, solitary shame
In memory of every mistake I learned—
that a flower barely opens before it gets burned
that a voice must miss its umpteenth turn
In memory I know
I stand
I show
in full view

Pre-serve

It's that self-preservation thing
that I-got-to-take-care-of-myself-first call
behind that unconscious invisible wall

it's that self-preservation thing
on top of that this-is-how-I-did-it-then stall
with
blinders on a repeat-the-past shawl
on top of that I've-got-to-fit-in-with-it-all
while I
breathe out of the side of my mouth trick
because the front of my mouth was ordered to quit
breathing that way is my salvation kit
do I have to keep that going forever?

it's that self-preservation thing
that small-bodied sing-along sing
that harmonize-even-if-it-hurts
while you squeeze into someone else's shirt
just to look like you're going the main road
show the light bag and hide the heavy load
and for god sakes don't reveal your travel mode
you stay alive if you stay the old code
what else ain't new?

it's that self-preservation thing
it takes more than the obvious to stay alive
when you live mostly in between the lines
self-preservation preserves all things contrived
preserves a place in the status quo hive
so you superimpose the almighty known
to stay safe in your preservation zone
it's familiar in your muted home

it's that self-preservation thicket
that turns into a stamped and sealed ticket to
silent and separate from your own heart
that's self-preservation
how did that start?

it's that self-preservation—great insurance
solid state replete with wall-to-wall deterrence
and you don't have to bother to apply
everyone got it from the same place
deep inside
lest you forget
then its self-preservation double standard
one for all/all for one face on two panderers
that's when self-preservation becomes the dismantler
until I remember what the self-preserved *all* do
to be as self-preserving as I am fool
like
the self-preservation couples' dance
locked up in convolution's romance
like
you care about me, don't you, in the end?
you sure act like you do
it's that
that bend
it's that all this time I thought I knew you
you never mentioned you were in it for yourself too
and in it with your own twisted rules

it's that ulterior high gear motion
paid for by a whatever-it-took-then token
to keep keeping despite all that erosion
don't let on you are the object of your own skewed devotion
if you want a date this weekend

and it's that let's-get-together-I-love-you
it's that there's-so-much-we-can-do
it's that I-trust-you-you-trust-me-too
it's that one-false-move-and-I'm-outta-here
zoom!

it's that watchdog barking at the moon
all day and all night
no matter what's obviously or not in sight
no matter

break it yourself before it automatically shatters

it's that time bomb
that age-old habit
it's that built in, self-made grab it!
that I-didn't-get-it-handed-to-me
I had to take it before anyone could see
it's that bow to the unruly queen and king
that self-preservation thing
presiding ad nauseam

so what of all that self-preservation going?
can't it happen without all that back-log towing?
how do you un-know all that knowing?
and all those fears
self-preservation wise
can be the kiss of death in a harmless flirt's disguise
safety in attractive numbers?
think again

there goes that self-preservation shard
hits you with a paradox
real hard
a gold carte blanche bottom-out card
am I spinning my wheels or what?

self-preservation doesn't have to be a grind
life per life
this life could be a find
if you're willing to flag down a little roadside service
real service
when your self-preservation has actually made you impervious
and all this time you put on like you were connected just to keep from
feeling rejected
now you discover that you and your lover are barely protected
from your own selves much less each other
something's got to give
you need more than that to live
and I mean more than crumbs
picked up with a tool of all thumbs

and I don't mean green ones
something's got to give

self-preservation
it's only natural
to assure yourself a place where you can catch it all
all that you need to stay intact
back and front
front and back
instead of straddling the line between past and current facts
and covering up all your feeling tracks
before *you* even track them
still
the track remains
for the time being
I'm bolted together by a rusty contraption
eating away at this stop/go action
hey! I fit in don't I?

self-preservation
common and ancient
curious to look calm and be delirious
self-preservation do and die
know the truth and spew the lie
that's self-preservation
I'll be damned
how did my survival get so jammed?

Dis-ease

There is a dis-ease
what's its name?
you name it
challenge
competition
I saw a little boy fall off his bike to the ground
his grandfather urged him to get up and ride around—
it's a challenge!
he said to the tender boy crying
with no arms extended
no patience
no finding
time to let him have his fall
or his feelings in the face of it all
get back on the bike
he must
or mommy's going to leave him in the dust
that's what she said
that's what she threatened
is this his mother?!
this fascist
this wretched
insensitive to her own dis-ease
yet instructing him to share that with her please
is this his mother?!
not in the classic sense
but typical to claim this role as defense
to treat this boy any which way
because she owns him doesn't she?!
she owns him

there goes another dis-ease
it started with an innocent pair of skinned knees
incubated in the middle of a park
where all things appear normal
years later
that boy will forget the dread that festered around him
those anaerobic germs that threatened to surround him

he'll build up his own resistance
to his vulnerable state's insistence
he'll forget how everybody slammed the gate on his emotions
he'll forget those emotions altogether
he'll forget how everybody *taught* him that the weather
should blow in dry and with a sunny smile
he'll forget his own heart after a while
what's it going to take to remind him of that
beautiful and fitting feeling state?
that place inside that eventually complies
to carry out its dis-ease fate

there is a dis-ease
what's its name?
you name it
challenge
competition
a healthy young man skate races in Florida
thinks nothing of a drunk dead in a corridor
he wears a politically correct shirt
and runs a fresh fruit and vegetable juice bar
climbs mountains
he's drinking freely from the fountain of "wholesomeness"
but what about that drunk
and all those others who are *really* sick?
this hunk
this young man
who looks good in a mirror
thinks he's fit and couldn't be clearer
that it's those others over there
he lives right
he couldn't be fairer
maybe he is
and maybe he's not
he cracked his chin on a hard spot
while skate racing and laughed it off with customers one day
what about his chin?
what of it?

he'd say—
it's just a chin
it's just sore muscles
I can push myself
it's a challenge
it's clean, fun competition

was this man once a boy
who never got permission
to travel along the line of a gently voiced decision
to sit with hurt feelings flying
to let them fly
no denying?
if he had gotten such assistance
his chin would have its due
its tending
and somewhere in a corridor
sprawled out on a dirty floor
a drunk man might have his mending

I know it sounds too pat
to say we're all connected
and we're all in this together
I know it takes a stretch to see the correlation
but I can't help feeling
what appears to be revealing
albeit a matter of degrees
no matter how it contrastingly measures
we're all living with the same dis-ease
call it competition
a culturally sanctioned division
between the heart and body
if we really felt our hearts inside
could we tolerate a world that's rotting?
and on the edge of being pulled out from under
it's hardly an unreasonably occurring wonder
that what is true
admit it or not

eventually delivers its thunder
no matter the size
small, incidental or proportionally wide
the scale is always seeking its balance
a tender moment—
it's the ultimate challenge
to take its necessary ride

Which Came First?

Pretty girl stands by the friendly horse
proud boy sits in his uniform
way up there
way up there
way up in the official saddle

pretty girl chats and flutters her eyes
the horse nods his head
and the uniformed guy
shares a bit of his enthusiasm and knowledge with her
he never went to college
but he had very special training
for that very special task
he's a proud boy in his uniform
who is he you might ask?

he's our bona fide mounted protector
our reminder that we are not safe
our friend
our keeper of peace and quiet
our talc in a world that chafes

so why do I flinch when I look at him
why do I not feel relief
why do these beat walkers and riders and drivers
evoke in me such grief?

and why are they here?!
these grim shadow stalkers
making out to be in control
who approved, assigned and directed
this particular type to that gesticulative role—
the flagger-down of justice
are they really dedicated to serving in my best interests?
what inspires them to hold such a job?
are they after just a pay check?
what pumps them up to an unruly mob?
is it exciting to lasso in a speeder
a killer

a vagrant or a cheater
to lock away an evildoer
a gone-off-the-deep-end
twisted spewer of all things contemptible and vile?
it's a good thing one side wears a uniform
otherwise I couldn't tell the difference after a while

well maybe some members of that special population
maybe some are of conscious intent
maybe some inherited the tendency to work in that direction
maybe some grew into that bent
maybe some bought the upholder of good deeds fable
maybe some were determined to turn the tables
after themselves being raked over the coals
maybe some grew tired of paying
and are compelled to be the collector of tolls
maybe some feel safer in such a position
to have the last word
the on-the-spot decision
when it comes to pedestrian affairs
maybe some are wholesome, good and upright
maybe all are bridges in the night
defiling the dregs from left to right
maybe I'm judging from afar
it's hard to decipher true motivation when they're
propped up in their monolithic car

but which came first—
the crook or the crook watcher
the complainer or the complaint?
which came first—
the lifter up off the floor or the vulnerable and faint?

either way let's turn it over
to those who ticket, warn, halt and apprehend
what better way to fob off an act of suppression
onto a job that purports to defend?

without the mutually sanctioned abyss guard
who rounds up and hurls the horrible
hard
who'd prune back all the outgrowths of our off-kiltered state?
if we had no on-going enforcers
would the underhanded take over at an unstoppable rate?
no, no never
silly me to endeavor to untangle such matters of course
how dare I doubt, try to define or question
the uniformed boy on his horse

Little "P"

I was a little perpetrator
short not stout
imitating the grown-ups who bossed me about
I was a little perpetrator
a partner in crime
mimicking my master
time after time
I was a little liver
of the narrow and dim
calculating my options
slimmer than slim
I was a little breather
who wanted to breathe
taking my air from under her sleeve
clutching her hem
watching her leave
offering my hem
to the next imitator of me

Who Bears Who?

Any idiot can have a baby
and many idiots do
it's idiocy, I think, to split yourself in two
unless you are one of the far between and few
who reproduces life just to see what it will do
no control
no projection
just guidance and protection
a highly spiritual task
accomplished only by those who refuse to don the mask
of relentless authority forcing blind conformity
onto the small and innocent
i.e. working out your own shit
in the guise of wiser and beneficent

I have experienced this
first hand
and it's horrific
the motives are hidden but specific
it's actually natural for the ignorant
to go after their resolve
not to say that it's not cruel to use another's life
to solve one's own pent-up troubles
but why bury your offspring in that mount of unconscious rubble?!
nothing could ever be accomplished that way
actually much has been accomplished—
a rampant display—
addiction and crime
a writer who compulsively rhymes
where does it all come from?
who's to say
I just know new life needs its own air every day

could it ever be possible for one to sign up for the job
as a humble quester
a person who elects, first, to be their own digester
of all that stuff stored up from before?
I get the feeling that child-bearing would be re-defined to the core

with *that* as precedence
and then how many, I wonder, would so emphatically chose
such an experience—
no agendas
no interference
with a child's own developing aspirations
where would the parents park their frustrations
of old unmet needs and ancient failed deeds?
how would they re-claim their once sacrificed selves
from traditional, imposing and petrified creeds
for spontaneous clear action?
could there ever be such an animal
free from repetitious contractions?
could there ever be such an animal upon whom
clearer conscience could fall?
could we interconnectors ever escape from it all
and be willing to meet face-to-face
without taking on the role of authority by projecting
weakness and need all over the place?!

Have I myself escaped such a beast, you might ask
have I ever elected to take on the task of conception
I must tell you at this point
I'm not writing this piece from that direction
but I don't have to have a baby to know all the tricks
I take that back
I just had one
pen and paper's *my* fix
I know how to project in my own stylistic way
parent or not
and I know how to manipulate people to mirror my sway
the only difference is
friends upon whom I mistakenly assign my own tangled mess
or those friends for whom I have modeled *their* dress
protect them I don't
I confess
I believe there's a difference though between projecting

onto a child or onto a friend
one has the power to take back their hour
the other must wait for years to mend
or regenerate transgression all over again

I Am My Own Child

There for you
where for who?
square with you
fair
there for you
where for who?
aren't we a pair

she's there
under the crease
waiting to be released
by me!
and she doesn't want to score
she doesn't want to impress anybody
she never did
what for

there for you
where for who?
square with you
fair
there for you
where with who?
we are a pair

she's there under the shelter
bombs falling
she learned to hide
she's there
give her a hand up to an unconditional ride
how many times until I do it?
how I abandon her in so many ways
I'm her parent now
I'm her parent
for the rest of our days
how many times until I do it?!
it's amazing how I go away
she's used to that
she waits and hopes

while I look elsewhere
she stays

there for you
square and true
where were you
she said
I've been waiting
in your heart
while you've been living in your head
we've been reaching for the stars
but it's us we need instead

there for you
split in two
how would I know
she disappeared every time they set her up
for their show
she didn't know how to articulate
wasn't free to say no to "no"
I grew up and did the same to her
wherever we go
I grew up
was ashamed of her
they taught me how to be her foe

there for you
here we two
I will stop repeating the damage that was done
but it might take me a while to learn to have fun

there for you
she is you
and you are now it
we looked everywhere for each other
it's time to sit

sit with it
be fit in it
be sure

you are hers
sit with it
don't quit on it
one and the same
she is yours

The Poet Begs The Question

I'm not going to rhyme
this time
not going to fit
in it
the rhyme and reason
to contain my pain
to start my heart
bring it in to begin
make a place to end
and demand a hand
round every bend
to insure with words
my safety

I don't need this rhyme
I can handle it myself this time
without these patterned words
emotional birds
flapping their wings to sing
a painful, chaotic, unwieldy song
but is it wrong
for me to want the form
to want to shield myself in an unpredictable storm
which way is it going to blow?
it's my way to lay low in a pen
better yet a pencil
to squeeze myself through the stencil
of words
pre-formed
pre-designed
it's there I find my holder
my sympathetic shoulder
but I can cry
I can be with a teary eye
I don't have to rhyme
this time
I don't have to take refuge in this body of words just to endure
I can find a way to stay with every feeling that comes into play
I can

It Wasn't Just A Dream

I went there
I went there and danced
I went there and danced naked
I went there and danced naked off the ground
I went there and danced naked off the ground
in the mirror
I went there and danced naked
off the ground in the mirror
of my mother's house
impossible
I could never get naked in my mother's house
I could never dance in my mother's house
I could never dance naked in my mother's house
or look at myself in the mirror
I could never dance in my mother's house naked in the mirror
in my mother's house and like
naked
and like what
and like what I
and like what I saw
never
I could never
but I did
I did dance naked off the ground in the mirror
in the naked mirror of my mother's house naked
and like
what I see
myself
I see myself
I like myself
I was myself
in her house
I am myself
in mine
in myself
naked
I liked myself naked

I went there naked and danced
really danced
really there
weightless
in perfect circles
spinning circles
ballet body
spinning around the stairway
the stairway in the middle of her floor
beautiful
beautiful ballet body
real body
spinning around her floor
and then I woke up

An Empty Vessel Abhors A Vacuum
—Fill It Yourself

Next time I ask you what you think or see or feel
about me
next time I ask you what you think or see or feel
about me
next time
there won't be a next time
that I ask you and decide that you know better what I should think, see
or feel
how I come across to you
is *your* deal
not mine
I have my own now
I am building my own so I can think, see and feel myself
the way I want to
because I know you see yourself when you look at me
there is absolutely nothing I can do to control what or how you perceive
me
you don't perceive me
you perceive you
and whatever it is you need or want to
if I ask and you tell me how I did with this or that
if I ask you and you tell me
I ask and you tell me
why do I ask you to jell me
I can coagulate myself

it always comes down to forgetting that you have your own agenda
everyone has to have their own agenda
it's a must
now I must have one too
so I can stop asking you
you are not my agenda broker
and I am not your client
I'm on my way to self-reliance
I'm on my way to asking myself what I see and think and feel
you are not in my way
I must start to listen carefully to everything you say

and accept graciously
what it is I need to learn from you and there is much to learn
to stop taking personally how you perceive what I say and do
I can approve of myself
I'd better as hell do that too
or I'll forever be looking to win your approval
all the while forgetting you have criteria
and forgetting to get at my own
then trying to win your approval
which is like betting against great odds
I could never win that race
I have never won that race
I don't want to enter that race
ever again
that old agenda of mine is dead
please please *me*

it would be a miracle if we intercepted and arrived at the same
point
the same place
the same feeling
the same investment
the same self
I know that one
I've done that one
I've done the merging
with those who raised me
and those who purged me of myself
as though I were unfit to live in here
I've recently returned
moved back into my own house
all uninvited guests are now invited to leave

it's amazing how people give me their opinions
I ask for them
I admit it
I invite their opinions
but somehow there's this agenda amnesia

so that when people give me their opinions
we both forget that their opinions are based on their own agendas
and they voice these opinions *honestly*—
"I say, in all honesty..." they say
as though we shared agendas
we used to
they had theirs and I had theirs
but I didn't really
I just wanted to impress severely
talk about chaos in a faithless world
if we recognized all the infinite possibilities
agendas brewing within the pot of probabilities
in a faithless world
it's too scary
in an ordered world
opinions are blaring and narrowing
and it seems they enter of their own volition
with insidious aggression
maintaining this impression that we are all as one
cultural incest
can penetrate the bone
cultural incest
don't answer the false phone
cultural incest drove me from my home
I have decided to inhabit it
more
then more
and that is good—
according to me
today I have the choice
but I must stay awake to make it

You Said So Yourself

So
did you like it?
did you really like it?
did you really really really really?
how much?
there I go again
looking for your touch
looking for your yes
looking for myself in your eyes
I can see myself slip into the small size
again
the small girl full of joy and love
back then
the small and meek
the small is still here

did you like it?
did you get it?
who is asking this question
who is wanting to know
I am going to go around the long way
several turnings off the wrong way
until I hear my own voice
until I listen to my own voice asking
myself
listen
I am asking for acknowledgement
I can give that to myself
now that I am living here
listening
now that I am living in this body of drawers
I want all of them to open so I can see what's in there
I can look for myself and see what's in there
I can be the miracle I am searching for
I can stop, look and listen
I can take the time and the care and concern
for all the things
to get all those things

that I have *learned* are impossible to get
I have looked for too long
with regret
outside
looking out there for those things
those gentle embraces
those trillions and zillions of *loving* nods
throngs of applause
that is my right to have
and I will have it
because I will give it to myself
as a certified adult
the one with the brains *and* the heart *and* the courage
yes, Dorothy
you always had the power yourself
yourself
you found them on the road
you lost them on the road
you *are* the road
your aunt was full of worry
your uncle
passive and full of fear
your other uncles
showed up to teach you how to steer
your own boat
say goodbye to the wizard
he was only there long enough to remind you that you forgot
and the monkeys took the wicked spot
the monkeys were yours too
and the witches and the munchkins in the land of you
and the journey
shook your foundations
spun you out and back
when you returned *home* it didn't really matter
that they didn't believe you

Standup Painedian

I know how to be funny
for money
I know how to be funny
you say you want me to be funny
while I am writing this book
or hurry up
you say
hurry up and be funny again
I know how funny you can be
how joyous and cute
someone should put you in a movie
you're so cute
be funny and gay
hurry
other people should know how funny you can
be funny

would you ask a bleeding soldier to be funny
to make jokes
before his blood clots?
would you tell him in the middle of it
that you remembered how funny he could be?
thank you Norman Cousins
I do believe humor is medicinal
I do believe in humor
pain gets the bad press
except *hip* pain of course
vogue pain
million seller pain
what about real pain
the kind that makes you *feel* pain
that's not funny
that's not stylish
unless you are removed enough to file it
and categorize it as such
if I show you my pain and my pain puts you in touch with your pain
and you don't want to feel your pain
don't ask me to be funny

I know funny
I was raised on funny
I ate, slept, breathed funny
I memorized Lenny Bruce material when I was eight years old
I recited Bruce material when I was eight years old
for my father and his friends
that was funny in my house
Lenny Goose was mother in my house
Lenny, Lenny Bruce
and Groucho and Gleason and Ball
and my carnal mother
was the funniest of them all
ghostly! her pain
god forbid we should bring it out in the open
she saved it for me
in the private corners
in my bath
I soaked in her tears
while she put on funny for everyone else
I don't like private pain
I don't like funny pain
cute funny
avoidance funny
but I know funny
I can do funny
I can tour funny on the hump of a mythical beast
I can tour on the hump with the best of them
the hump feels like home
I return there again and again
I have mastered that ride and ask when
when will my pain be taken seriously
when will my pain be allowed to stand up and be counted
I am counting on my pain to relieve itself by the very
fact of its apparent existence
the close, intimate fact
not the fact of explosions and violent storms
and ungodly statistics

it's the quiet
the invisible
the ungross
the latent
the kind that can be contacted in a minute
a direct real minute
not so far removed to be too far to fathom
a direct real minute that pain
frighteningly funny isn't it—
no
it's not frightening or funny
it just is.

I Don't Use Matches

Is it happening again it isn't happening again is it happening again it can't happen again I fixed it so it won't happen again but it's happening again what's happening again NO POWER she said I NO POWER she said I can't use NO POWER she said I can't use the phone NO! I need to use the phone is it happening again it isn't happening again is it happening again it can't happen again I fixed it so it won't happen again but it's happening again what's happening again NO POWER she said she NO POWER she said she would NO POWER she said she would meet me she said she would meet me here she said she would meet me here at one o'clock she said NO POWER she said NO POWER she no show NO POWER NOOOOOOOOOOOOOOO!

I went walking POWER walking hard and hard and harder and louder I screamed on the circle on the round return of my small no power body that wanted to scream and was told she couldn't in so many in *no* many in *no* words in *no* looks in *no* deeds in *no* scapegoat *no* threats *no* eyes *no* body language told she couldn't so she wouldn't even know that she couldn't scream that she wanted to scream that she wanted to have power is it happening again it isn't happening again is it happening again it can't happen again I fixed it so it won't happen again but it's happening again NOOOOOOOOOO I am not small anymore NOOOOOOO I don't want to feel small anymore NOOOOOOOOO I feel small I feel so small I want to scream I have to scream NOOOOOOOOOOOOOOO I fixed it NOOOOOOOOO I fixed it so it won't happen anymore I don't want it to happen anymore ever again!

I went home the phone rang he knew it was a wrong number he knew it was a wrong number he knew my name he spoke my name I asked him how he knew my name he laughed why did I feel ashamed for asking he knew my name and said he had the wrong number NOOOOOOOOOOO I hung up NOOOOOOOOO the phone rang I let the machine answer the phone rang I let the machine answered and someone that I knew was leaving a message about a show about half-price tickets about please buy about buy this about I should about cough up about buy some buy money buy this about buy buy buy quiet I will sleep now I will check out of this no power no show no buy too try too too no no power no no show no phone bad phone wrong phone buy phone sleep at home sleep it off sleep off power off anger off rage off liver burning inside the no power body the *no* body the invisible kick and scream body the lift the granite house of cards body lift the boulder house of rage feathers floating down incidental and powerless and incidentally the phone rings again it couldn't be him there wouldn't be time has passed too much time to repeat that crass I pick up the phone and no one is there but a–click–the phone rings again I let the machine answer the machine plays the machine goes the machine blank dead moving dead sound space moving on the tape on escape I fixed it I didn't pick it up I don't have to pick it up I can fix it I can't fix how do I trick it so it never happens again?

the package comes the package says I have to do it myself and they will get the pay off they said I have to do it all do it most and they will do some and they will do little and they will get more than me and they will get much more than me because they are big they are bigger they are stronger they have more resources they have more people they have more money they have more power more position because they have been here longer and why can't I be stronger and why must I work my butt off a zillion times more that's what it seems like a katrillion times more and they will this and I won't that and that is how my day started and the woman who didn't show owned me money too!

I sat down with my loaded gun fingers on the keyboard I sat down and shot my mountain on the mountain load the mountain shot my mountain I went to my corner I rose from my corner I fought in my corner I won I won the fight because I will speak the fight shriek the fight is wrestled down with big strong tangible visible audible feelable unmistakable paper fists

and they will be read and they will show and they will throw
their punches out into the field of ears giant ears earhearts
lending beating leaning in my direction in my big body smart
body option body scream body now body now leaning beating
yes YES to my fingers yes to my anger yes to my body yes to me
yes said my fingers yes said me!

are arson fires set off by people with *no* fingers?

Dear Yesterday

How to not take it personally
take it personally
how to not take it personally
take it personally
take it personally
take it shake it quake it
into
unto yourself
and hold yourself responsible
totally and completely
for every error
every first, last and middle error
every mishap that befalls you
every misunderstanding that galls you
every injustice and glitch and twitch that passes before your eyes
it's you who are to be criticized
you
you and your ways
every minute of your days
it's you
turn around and look
hold your arms open as you throw the book
at yourself
you did it
you flubbed it
you wrecked it
you blew it
they knew it
intuit the truth
it's you
your fault
your failing
your flaw
it's time you got it together
and comprehended the law that reads
when something happens that disappoints you
it's time to pay because

you did it wrong
you'd better do something about this
you'd better change yourself
you'd better *do* something
you'd better control things that are out of your control
you'd better take it personally

when something happens outside of yourself that you have absolutely
no control over
and if that no control event came and went
unexpectedly
and un-preferably
it's time to take it personally
a perfect pretense for control
take it personally
take that role
and roll it around until outside circumstances switch
and pull you out of the personal ditch
in time to see
that you don't have to take it personally
or as a direct reflection
unless you need to view your projection
of yourself in a contrived state
wrapping yourself in something familiar
something that says you've got a handle on it
when in fact you're in a boat
a rocky, unstable, moving boat
off and away from shore
you can stop this motion
you can say no more
just take it personally
take control
or
go back out to sea
and let the waves of surprise and transformation
put you in touch with the little me
the little me who wanted to fix it

because the little me had needs
and couldn't bear the thought that
everybody had needs
conflicting
everybody had needs and all of them were outside of control
the little me couldn't concede
or understand how larger forces are going to mix it
and how nobody on earth could ever fix it
but the little me believed
so she took it personally
just like you take it now
so now becomes then and you're back to
take it personally all over again
until you can't take it personally anymore
because you walked through another door marked *UNKNOWN*
and made it

there now
feel better?
the big you and little me meeting up again
just to be told
that it takes two and even two are not exactly running this show
Love, You
P.S. Everything is going to be all right

Do You Recognize Her?

If I speak of the ghost
will you run and hide
will you think I am crazy deep inside
will you look at me with that far-away stare
with that look that says *I* am out there

If I speak of the ghost
will you force me to sit in the corner
again
play the mourner
and then say—
I see no dead body here
no coffin
no covered mirror
no fruit baskets
no visitors
why are you crying?!

If I speak of the ghost will you rear up and gallop away
while I stand in the middle of the barren field
trying to lift the laden echo of my self
up into my heels
into my feet
my legs
my pelvis
my sweet
small waist
and all the rest
my skull
and face

If I speak of the ghost
will you know I was chased into the hollow
wanting to swallow
something
anything
other than its relentless fist
planting itself into the gist of my entire existence
from day one

when a murdered woman bore me
and then murdered me
a murdered woman bore me
and murdered me
bore me and murdered me
and left no evidence
except for the ghost
the ghost and myself—
its host

the ghost knows
the ghost travels
the ghost carries a timeless gavel
it has been pounding in my heart to speak of it

If I speak of the ghost will you know that I really
don't want to dig up the muck
I've spent my life trying to duck out of its way
trying to tuck myself into the splay
of sweet mother flesh instead
but there was none
no sweet mother flesh
in no one
but the ghost
the ghost in me is harbored
I must carry it
I must nurse its wounds by my own sweet flesh
I must bear it
I swear it is mine to speak of

I will speak of the ghost
I will speak to see
to speak of the ghost is to speak me

Triplet

Before the dancing begins
I must consecrate the music
before the dancing begins
I must bathe my frozen feet
before the dancing begins
I must promise not to cheat myself of every note
this time
and flex my throat so that it can stretch across the dream's horizon
lift up sound
call itself around to awakening
every step will be heard
every muscular word
bending forward with letters outstretched
and sentences pointing to dance
and the dance conjoining to music that was once played
by a deaf musician for a catatonic ballerina
this music is new
I want to hear it and move
this time

before the dancing begins
I must unwrap my legs like an infant
soft
slow
exposing only the bare minimum at first
for fear that the worst will happen

before the dancing begins
I dance privately
rehearsing the volatile rhythms for naught
because the practiced dance is not the dance itself
the music is changing
the dance is unavoidable and cannot be anticipated
my feet are not employable for the old and dangerous
dance that never was
this dance is different
it is
constructed toe by toe

grown to show itself
by way of a *near* Biblical promise, sturdy ankle and a willing heart

I Rite Myself Passage

This book will come with no instructions
so handle it with care
because you're reading about yourself
although it's my words in there
my details
my specifics
my facts and figures
please don't look to me if you're triggered
look within

this book will come with no interpreter
or engineer for static control
no seeing eye dog to steer you around blind corners
if you misunderstand my words
or think of me as wrong for writing them
I say you are strong for inviting them into your view
the act of reading them is just as imbued as
the very words themselves
the reason why I wrote them may not be the reason why you
tote them home
but never mind
no matter
I can't control the latter
nor can I control the result
criticism or credit
I can only catch the drift from my direction
and release myself from *other* perceptions
I'm doing what it is I have to do
from the audience of myself first

and we needn't speak of it as art
this work is worlds apart from unconscious projections
acceptance or rejection cannot be my aim
my motives here are not the same
as one who creates art for a living
I live for a living and then record it
so don't lord over it
because this book happens to be for sale

going public is a preoccupational hazard—
the spilling over of poured water
the conspicuous transformation of an invisible daughter
buying or selling a heart's return record
means more than it seems to entail
and more than can ever be explained
suffice it to say
this book does come with love
and no small plea for you to read in its name

Testimony

I don't want to rock the boat
but it has a hole in it
I don't want to rock the boat
I don't want to rock the boat
but it isn't taking me where I want to go
I don't want to rock the boat
but it's sinking
it's not just the hole
in my mind I am thinking
how you said you love me and I wanted to believe
you said you love me and I say
leave love to the lovers
the boat rockers who
paddle with a real
hard paddle
it is so hard to know that I cannot accept this love you offer
that I cannot be your daughter anymore because
to be your daughter is to be required to accept this offer
and to accept it is to
die
not for dramatic effect
I am not writing for dramatic effect
I wish to be direct
but is it possible to speak as someone who is no longer the person that
you once knew
and be heard?
please don't offer me
the 'L' word
because I know what it means and you refuse to

I can't write my mother so I am writing a book
I can't write my mother or any member of my family
honestly
and honestly tell them what I have to say
in this newly acquired
dare I require it?
language
because it cannot be understood by the emotionally illiterate

I don't want to rock the boat
emotion illiteracy
I don't want to rock the boat
is a terrible heart to waste
a terrible heart is a silenced heart
and a forthcoming heart
dare I say is
how dare I display it for the whole world to see?
to pronounce my heart is to renounce my part
my daughterhood
and quite possibly be put in contempt of court
so sue me
I am on the stand as the true me
love is something in common we
could have if you renounce your daughterhood too
is that something you'd be willing to do with me
to drop the roles that demand I belong to you and you belong to her and
she...
instead of ourselves?!
I am writing this to stay awake
I am writing this because the words help me to paddle

in her letter she said she loved me
she said she loved me as my mother
and I wanted to believe
as the boat went down
I started to grieve
is her love contingent upon this little girl disappearing again?
said the lawyer to the defense
is her love stringent?
said the evidence in the light
is her love historically harmful?
I rest my case

please know that I want to love and be loved as ourselves
if you insist upon playing mother
I must tell you not to bother because the role has been given to someone
else

a permanent casting
true to type and everlasting
it took years to get *my* court to award the role to me
and I have accepted

as I exit the boat
I find I am floating in 65% of myself

Getting My Feet Wet

There
I'm done
I'm whole
I'm together
I think I'll step outside and check the weather
whoops!
it looks pretty harsh out there
it feels pretty crude
it appears the machine is still pumping up exceedingly
distasteful food
I don't have to eat it
but I am not entirely immune
how do I connect with "out there" and continue to be in tune
with myself
knowing that I am on a more than slightly different track
and not without lack for
or shall I say not without absence of desire
to mingle without pretense
and feed my social fire
I had better not require much
in the way of frequent commendations
or random explanations
for the inexplicable life I lead
I have to be very careful about where I direct my needs
and how I read them

it's amazing how when I come from that place
that undeliberated extension
that seemingly inexhaustible resource that hangs off
that all-knowing, mysterious dimension
it's like a gentle tap on the shoulder
an immediate soul unfolder—
subliminal traffic light
stop!
somebody is speaking to you with their own motives
look!
they haven't the faintest notion of what yours are
listen!

discover your own
they needn't be on par with anybody else's
they just need to be known
by you

what a wacky concept
to be my own best friend
who on earth would ever encourage me to be conscious as I tend
to my own garden
and nourish from my own roots
where in the world can I find such a person
besides myself
who aims to protect all those independent shoots
that spring forth from the sturdy soils
where delicate and gentle reside
amidst the coarse
the subtle and fine seldom *seem* to be what all decides
how things are out there
rough and offensive
to a plethora of natural wonders
including myself who would never knowingly commit or encourage
such awful and heavy blunders
water would never botch itself
nor would the air
unlike natural disasters
there seem to be forces that *deliberately* don't care
or just do not know how to
and though I'll always be interdependent
I will pick up my own and plow through this looming legacy
and hope as I go in my direction
I meet others along the way
as I reach out to only myself for permission
to say what I know to say

This Blame Thing's Got To Go

If a person accidentally shoots off my foot
wouldn't it be reasonable for the doctor to ask
"how did this happen?"
should I say,
"it just happened."
or should I say,
"if I didn't have a foot this never would have happened."
or should I say,
"how did what happen?"
or should I say,
"it wasn't their fault the gun went off."
or
"OUCH!"
should I say ouch?
may I say,
"OUCH!"
and pray this never happens again
could I rest with the prayer
or rest *after* I tell the doctor how and where
this atrocity happened?
and might I have a strong urge to get the gun away from the gun shooter
so that my other foot can feel safe?
what if everybody, *accidentally*, is shooting off feet all over the place
and losing a foot is a common daily occurrence
and what if shutting up about is encouraged and the way to be thought
of as a noble, respectful and courageous soul?
I'd be hard-pressed to convince anybody to say
it hurts to have your foot shot off
but it does hurt and pain's a curious thing
especially if you are awake to it
feelers of pain want to know
where did it come from and how to get it to go away for good
would you tell a footless person that she should be quiet about her pain
and that to identify the source of it is to, well, god-forbid, to blame
and "blaming is not right"
so she must "forgive with all your might"
but I am in pain

and I want it to end
and I would like to use my might for myself
to prevent it from happening again
how might I do this in a world of sleeping-ankled, foot blamers
in a world of gun preferrers and trigger-happy anger tamers?
how might I do this
in a world where mute one-footed people are taken for granted
because two-footed people are so rare?
and most everybody has forgotten that two feet are even possible
and to keep more than one is highly improbable
so losing one is nothing to bear
and therefore nothing to guard
but it is natural to be self-protective
in a jungle the lion roars
in the city of one-footed strangers
we smile and quietly lock our doors

A Forked Tongue Begets A Forked Tongue

I saw her in the post office
she was tugging at the bow on her pant cuff
her mother said, "don't pull on your bow—
you don't want it to come off."
wait a minute here
I thought to myself
wait a minute about this want
who is who and who doesn't want this decorative feature
to be disassembled?
I had a feeling the child's opinion on the subject
had not as yet come into being
so why didn't the mother call it in accordance
with what the truth itself was seeing
as in "I don't want the bow to come off
so don't pull on it for me"
a straightforward demand—
honest as honest could be
it's those little details that build up
and become increasingly slippery
I'm sorry little girl for not speaking up on your behalf
failing to outrightly identify the wheat from the chaff
I wonder how many times people will insert their opinion into you
until you forget or barely form your own
what can be done to prevent these occurrences from turning your sense-
abilities to stone?

I saw him by the berry bush
standing on his toes
his mother picked a piece for him
he expressed what his senses told
"sour?" she said
"you're getting picky"
picky?! I thought
what a critical reaction
how about commending the boy for speaking up on his taste buds' behalf
and for outrightly identifying the wheat from the chaff
but if she feels his expression of taste is somehow a criticism of her
then expressing his taste becomes a troublesome chase between what he

can and cannot prefer
after a while what he knows and what he shows will summarily be
disengaged
including his knowledge that in that moment her hand was filled with
berries *and* rage
I'm sorry little boy for not applauding your accurate perceptions out loud
as you called a spade a spade
and I'm sorry for not untangling that stifling deception thrust upon you
you are not picky for recognizing and expressing that which you
recognize
not picky in *her* way
hopefully after zillions of these experiences
you can emerge free from who on this day you are—
a boy being raised by a woman who picks fruit to be put in a jar
with a tight lid

Parenting Requires No License and Issues No License

It all started in a friendly restaurant
amidst friendly people
talking, laughing
eating tasty food with pleasing smells—
a little boy
able
to open his mouth and emit sounds between sips of juice
audible sounds
happy sounds
I am alive! sounds
disturbing apparently only to his mother
who elected to use her fingers as a cover
a handy gag
not to smother his breath
just his vocalization of joy—
sounds as harmless as this little boy

I looked upon her smothering
and wondered what in the name of silence she was uttering
and how many times she censored him in this way
and what her censorship had to say
to him
as I looked upon this scene I saw it as disturbing
and utterly grim
and I saw myself unable to bang the table and scream stop!
which is exactly what I felt like doing
but I sat there and watched and froze
I chose to censor myself
I chose
to rather than take the chance of being misunderstood—
evoke anger and defensiveness or be told that I should
mind my own business
I chose to sit by and lose the chance to squelch mute in the making
I felt myself weak and weakened more in the forsaking
of what I know and believe so strongly to be true
this woman
as mother

or person
had no right to do what I saw her do

nobody but me seemed to notice this seemingly casual
parent/child affair
was I making a mountain out of a molehill?
still
icebergs start with one drop of water
a redwood begins with a seed
a single sound grows into a symphony
next time I see someone cutting off the flow of living, true, direct,
harmless expression
I will step forward and make my utmost confession:

I see what you are doing
I know what it's construing
you cannot hide your intention
to control the defenseless for your comfort's sake
you are not respecting this boy's rights
to celebrate life with his vocal tones
if you are uncomfortable
acknowledge your discomfort as your own
I have a feeling his vocal output is not the sole prompting
of your decision to gag him
if you cannot be emotionally responsible
as in
able to respond to your own emotions without hampering
someone else's
parenting
if it hasn't already will become problematic
you cannot control your kids forever
or any outside source that fails to insure your comfort level
there is something besides his mouth in desperate need of
uncovering
pop the lid on your discomfort and let the boy express himself
the stopping of one won't prevent the other
the allowing of both will allow you to discover
something of value with its own tone

calling out to be called your own
something—

I cannot describe it
I think I've said enough
confessing my reactions to her is tough
and much easier to write down on paper
but someday I will confide directly out
from inside
as soon as I clear my throat of my mother's finger

Or Could We?

If all the people are merely players
I would like to meet us all backstage
costumes off
props down
scripts dispensed with
and I would like to have a giant cast party
everyone invited
to celebrate the show being over
curtain dropped
end of run
no more reviews

we could laugh about the slights of hand
pretense
and illusions grand
the grandest
and the acting out—
superb!!

we could warm up to one another
victims and evildoers could be lovers
delighting in each other's actual presence
knowing exactly how the script pulled our strings
manipulating us to do outrageous things
on stage
for the audience's cries and entertainment
we could thank the skies for covering the stage for our containment
upon which to depict every raw emotion under
crimes, deceits and split devotions
intrigues to captivate, horrify and amuse
all action prompted by none other than the director's cues
knowing full well that what we have done
was based upon someone else's notion
we would never chose to really participate in such obviously
dire commotion
if it all were true
and if it were
we could never unify the entire cast

or have the drama enlighten us all
at last
we could never congratulate all of us, with love, for making such a
terrific show
or say,
"good—
you played the finest arrow
evil—
you portrayed a most rigid bow
audience—
you shook in your boots as they stood toe to toe"
we could never say it was fun to suspend disbelief
to perform the age-old tale of duality
we could never thank the author for such palpable grief
and say—
"good job,"
with relief
"come on now, let's all get back to reality!"

May I Be Excused?

I don't identify with the killer
it's true
the sharp-featured
long-fingered
shifty-eyed
boxed-eared
the three-piece-suited
uniform-geared
the martial artist
mafia-steered
the money monger
corporate clique
alley loitering
do-it-quick
dirty-fingered
hired hand
I don't identify with the killing land

but I have killed
in quiet moments
I have killed
with little notice
weapon-pointed
with accurate focus
a heart laid down before me
I have killed
and left no marks
to match my own invisible scars
it's a clean cut
exempt from bleeding
easy prey
always conceding to an angry will
never needing much in the way of ammunition
averting look
a missed touch
dismissing tone
missing much
in the way of close contact

I kill and I witness the killing
I am my primary victim and suspect

with much practice on myself
those who come close best be armed
I kill best at close range
traps set with my charm
I've been known to endear myself quickly
wielding plenty of personal power
on my best behavior
I don't get dangerous until the start of the intimate hour
and when the clock strikes subtle
when armour melts away
when my victim begins to resemble my very first prey
I load up on my best-of tapes
the DJ of fear starts to play
I spin out on the tenderest of feelings
the ones that come the closest to those I am concealing

"kill them,"
says a voice from within "before they kill you—
kill them—you have been taught from the start—
do to others what's been done to you"
no mess
no gore
no pre-meditated fussing
what for?
murdering a heart requires little to no discussing
no legalities or concrete proof
no front page or prime time news
a mere tree falling in an empty forest

when the killing's done
and I can count the consequential losses
I round up all the casualties
and identify their causes
I reach out, in earnest, to my opposing soldier
"stand up straight,"
says our commander

"pass yourself through your own heart's border
or guard it with an iron block
while you wait for your next killing order"

I don't identify with the killer—
sloppy technique
so backwards and crude
murdered hearts are barely recognizable *before* they are murdered
I can't identify with the killer
I refuse to sit at the same table with one
I'd be caught dead sharing the spoon of my not so distant cousin

Nonnegotiable

There is no debate when it comes to my feelings
I won't argue pros and cons
I won't take the stand to spell out my defense
I can't protect your ears
or dispel your fears
there's nothing to be gained by apologetic lip service
or your guilt-ridden recompense
there is no rationale
no right or wrong
no *let's be pals*
or good advice
or practical comparisons
there is no reason to be excused—
no *calm downs, take it easys,*
no *snap out of it—he was well meanings*
no children are willing participants in their abuse!
no *it was for your own goods*
no *forget the pasts, get on with its, you'd bests, you shoulds*
what's it going to take if you can't measure it
if no machine can weigh the treasure of it?
what's it going to take to see, hear and taste
that which you feel?
I cannot prove, convince, impress upon you what is real
and you cannot stop it
feelings persist and outlast it all
no matter how you try to drop it
they cannot be erased or covered over
for very long
the energy behind them is infinitely strong
they can be stilted with a ploy
or transform a puppet to a boy
they can be described or fablized
they can be drugged to "stabilize"
they can be twisted, mangled
subdued or squarely denied

I would like to share some with you
but I know you will try to talk me out of them

did you know that's tantamount to telling me I need no air
go ahead, tell me
tell yourself the same
I tell you a feeling-deferred world looks like a deoxygenated brain
but never mind, let's construct a lot of theories to keep that going
overtalk could never undermine the feelings that are knowing
they don't need your greenhouse to keep them growing
they don't even need me

Beloved Curtain Of Grief

Invite your anger to dinner—
breakfast, lunch, tea and a snack
hold it in your arms
rock it in your lap
feel it like a warm soft sweater feels your arms inside its sleeves
breathe through it like a sturdy wind
rustling through bright red leaves
be possessive, be selfish with it
give it your full attention
anger ignored is like water held
there is bloating from retention
puffing up the psyche
like a boulder hanging in suspension
welcoming it after long last
reduces its mammoth proportions
and prevents it from sending your mouth, ears, eyes and feet
back into heavy contortions

after you share a meal
and a one-on-one interlude
and after you watch it lower itself down
in front of yourself and a witness or two
thank your anger for sustaining itself
patient under your pillow
nudging you awake in the shade of your trusty weeping willow
where all feelings are acceptable

Equal Time/Moot Point

Parents as people who abuse power
need no more support for what they do
they have readily whole cultures behind them
we need no search party to find them
they are all over the map
parents as people who abuse power
don't need to have a scheduled hour during which to be represented
these great in number have voice most everywhere and by their numbers
are automatically defended and protected and made to feel comfortable
thanks to all of us mutes in hiding
the truly endangered species
holed up in our subdividing
loyal to our first priority
those who pronounce seniority—
those with the *power* to punish or provide
parents as people who abuse power are hard-pressed to be denied
and we the endangered species would rather die than show our truth
and we are dying to show it
we'll die if we don't
we have nothing at all to lose
except fear

With Absolute Pitch

In a perfect world the truth doesn't hurt
and everyone can afford to tell it
in a perfect world the truth doesn't hide
everyone can smell it
and say so
in a perfect world the truth waves like a flag
never required to lay low
in a perfect world we can trust the truth
because it lives within the heart
and everyone knows it is out of that place
all actions grow or tear apart
in a perfect world

in a perfect world
we rely upon the truth to be an accurate compass
leading us all to the main symphony hall
not a back room filled with discordant rumpus
in a perfect world the truth is never asked to say that it is sorry
because everybody understands the language must spell out its justifiable
real true story
and everyone listens to the story
as it is told
eager to know
eager to tell it with their own unbridled spontaneity
eager to wear it like a charm to keep us out of harm's way
in a perfect world the truth is not the catalyst for angry or fearful
reactions
but one giant bath drawn to warm and be shared by cold warring
factions
in a perfect world the truth adds up
never figures by subtractions
in a perfect world
the truth decides

Epilogue

July 3, 1994

Dear Mom,

I am glad that you wrote me. Our estrangement has been a difficult event in my life. I say event because it is part of a whole range of experiences I have been having and will continue to have—CHANGE! All my relationships are changing and I don't see how the relationship I have with you could be any different—especially since it is by far the most influential of all. I have thought of you often and have wondered what direction things would take between us.

I appreciate your acknowledging that I had pain growing up. However, you are not responsible for the feelings and perceptions I have about my own childhood. I am responsible for them. And that is what I have been doing since the last time we have heard each other's voices, Thanksgiving '91—I have been and continue to be developing the ability to comprehend, allow for, be response-able for my feelings. To me, this is a celebration of life not a "tragic unhappiness". I have suspected that you and, perhaps, other family members who, in the void of the absence of contact, have been left with the impression that I am sitting around lamenting or brooding or resenting childhood. Quite the contrary, I have been allowing my childhood feelings to surface so that I can integrate them and become more evolved as a human being with a full spectrum of emotions. I do not see my life as a "tragic unhappiness." There have been some tragedies and some unhappinesses but when I put it all together, tragedies and unhappinesses are only a part of the whole.

I never doubted that you did the best you could. The fact remains I did have feelings that went unacknowledged. I have learned, in my fervent quest to understand my own life experiences, how important it is for me to acknowledge my feelings whatever they are, regardless of your optimum efforts to parent me. One does not cancel out the other.

I am very proud of my efforts to understand myself and I am very proud of my development as a writer. I am about to publish a book that documents my process. It took me a year to write the main part of the book and about six months to write the author's note or introduction to it. I would like to send you a copy of the author's note because it explains the intention of the book and the premise out of which I continue to write about my personal and general observations which I think are very important. Writing about what I feel is true is my way of contributing to the solution. For me to not write would be contributing to the problem.

Writing the book was very much about my own personal process and a way to acknowledge the voices of my past. But writing the book is also about my adult life as a writer—someone who has learned from my past and developed the ability to articulate those things that people are either afraid or unable to articulate. I have done many readings from my book and that's part of what has informed me that my writings have a reason to be outside of my own insulated, often isolated, world. Nine individuals are financially sponsoring the printing of this book and many of the individuals who attended my readings have expressed great interest in obtaining the book. I am telling you this because I want you to understand that this book is, paradoxically, a difficult celebration—a difficult labor—and the offspring— my more vital existence that can assist others' vitality. The kinds of things that went on in my childhood not only went on in other childhoods but STILL GO ON TODAY and I refuse to sit in silence about my understanding of things that simply don't have to continue! It has become my life's work to observe and write on the way people do and could relate to each other.

You acknowledged that I had pain as a child. Thank you! Would you like to know the details of that pain? I know that reading this book, for you, would not be easy. The fact remains, I am on the threshold of seeing my book in print and made available to the public. It is up to me to give myself complete permission whether or not you approve and whether or not it would be easy. I know full well that reading my book would bring you a certain amount of discomfort. (Actually it could bring many people a certain amount of discomfort—but it's a good kind of discomfort because hiding from the truth is, ultimately, the least comfortable and the most dangerous and destructive). I know one thing for sure—it is very important for me as a person and as a professional writer to see this book in print. It is the riskiest thing I have ever done and the preliminaries have been the most rewarding.

I never thought it would be possible to have an active relationship with you AND do the kind of work I am doing—telling the truth as I see it. I am willing to try to do both. I am willing to explore uncharted territory.

Again, I thank you for making contact.

w/ ♥,

Pamela

Notes

In generating the pieces in *Speak Of The Ghost*, I began to understand an assortment of ways in which common everyday language alternately functions to corroborate whole self-acceptance or stifle it, and how the half-conscious use of language can and does perpetuate repressive mentality. In proofing my manuscript, I noticed that I used certain terms and attitudes that could reflect that mentality and do not necessarily reflect my current level of emotion literacy. To preserve the integrity of my spontaneous flow of writing and corresponding level of emotion fluency, I did not revise or "correct" the original text. With the exception of changing a tiny handful of words, alterations were applied to punctuation only. To cite a few examples of the fluctuating discrepancy between language and emotion literacy, for my own peace of mind and the optimum utility of this book, I found it necessary to footnote *I Never Knew* and *Voluntary Plea*.

[1] *I Never Knew,* page 24

> "but the child long ignored/always evens the score/by taking much more than your health"

It is not the long-ignored (or buried) child who takes your health but the burying that puts health in jeopardy.

[2] *Voluntary Plea,* page 87

> "I ask the child for forgiveness/don't *you* ask the child to forgive"

As discussed in the author's note, forgiveness is problematic when trying to sustain conscious contact with a full range of responses to past and current abuse, including anger. I used this term ironically, to express my developing awareness of having internalized the abuse and how apologetic I felt to myself. (See also the author's note, footnote 1, page *xix*.)

Suggested reading—books by Alice Miller including:

Banished Knowledge—Facing Childhood Injuries

*The Untouched Key—Tracing Childhood Trauma
in Creativity and Destructiveness*

*Breaking Down The Wall Of Silence—The Liberating Experience
Of Facing Painful Truth*

Index

of Titles and *First lines*

About The Author

Pamela Sackett conceived *emotion literacy* in 1992. She uses it to name, affirm and foster a level of awareness capable of reading, acknowledging and integrating the full spectrum of one's own personal context inherent in all human interaction. Some of *her* interaction includes protesting the war as an Ohio State and Kent State student (1970-72), composing and performing as a coffeehouse songstress, half a comedy team, and as a guru disciple on the road with a dancer. She took a break in a San Francisco psych ward, played the role of a delusional street person in an award-winning educational film, wrote artist profiles as a columnist for Pacific Northwest newspapers, questions for a game show, and designed plays and monologues for actors, high school drama students and mentally and emotionally ill individuals.

Some of her writing and teaching projects have been funded by the Seattle Arts Commission, King County Arts Commission, US West, the Metropolitan Arts Commission of Portland and the Seattle Repertory Theatre Company. Her original monologue book trilogy for actors entitled *Two Minutes To Shine* is published and internationally distributed through Samuel French, New York.

Presently, Pamela Sackett lives, writes and teaches in Seattle, Washington.

ELA™ *Order form*

Speak of the Ghost—In The Name of Emotion Literacy
by Pamela Sackett

Price $15.95 US   ISBN 0-929904-03-6

Quantity: ___ x $15.95 US =   _____

Less 5% for 5 or more books =   _____

Subtotal   _____

Sales tax (Washington state residents)   _____

Postage and Handling   _____

US/Canada: $2.50 US for one book, plus $0.50 for each
additional book. Allow 3-5 weeks for delivery.

International: $3.50 US for one book, plus $1.00 for each
additional book. Books will be shipped surface book rate.

Total   _____

Ship to:

Name   _____

Address   _____

City, State & Zip   _____

Phone   _____

Please send the full amount in check or money order to:

  Emotion Literacy Advocates™
  PO Box 95126, University Station
  Seattle, WA 98145-2126

Booksellers: please write for discount ordering information.